"*Spouse in the House* combincti-
cal marriage advice and hum   lby
weave together wit, wisdom,   ole
way to help everyone from i.   y .... .. long-marrieds have a
marriage that is enriching and joyful. Married for over forty years
with a SITH (spouse in the house) of my own, I found myself
highlighting insightful tips and doable strategies, chuckling out
loud, and nodding in agreement as I made my way through this
enjoyable read."

Shel Harrington, humorist, family law attorney, and author of
Over 50, Defined

"I just finished *Spouse in the House* and wrote seventeen pages of
application for our marriage of thirty-eight years! I wish I'd had
this book in the early days of my marriage when I struggled to
maintain togetherness without losing my individuality. Becky and
Cynthia's authentic stories, as well as the attitude adjustments and
practices they suggest, have moved me to action already. What a
treat that the authors talk back and forth about common issues
in marriage and have their husbands contribute too. This book
is a sheer gift!"

Tammy McLeod, Harvard chaplain and coauthor of *Hit Hard*

"With their incredibly vulnerable, well-researched, and often
mirthful writing, Cynthia Ruchti and Becky Melby provide a
timely and timeless resource for anyone who wants to improve
their relational life. The wisdom and practicality of *Spouse in the
House* applies to more than just marriage, but to 'everything God
wants to see happen in a church, in the world, . . . in families
and couples.'"

Dr. Patrick McLeod, Harvard chaplain and coauthor of
Hit Hard

"For twenty-three years, my husband and I have shared our work space as we've each run a business from home. I'm clear about the challenges our situation creates. Yet Cynthia Ruchti and Becky Melby's new book gave me renewed hope that perhaps we'll both make it out alive—and well. With candid humor, the authors share laugh-out-loud stories, great resources, and tips from a myriad of friends who know the life-sucking potential of all that closeness. Whether you're living the togetherness dream or anticipating it with dread, don't miss *Spouse in the House*!"

Deb DeArmond, coauthor of *Don't Go to Bed Angry: Stay Up and Fight!*

"*Spouse in the House* says it all. With honesty, humor, warmth, and wisdom, Cynthia Ruchti and Becky Melby give encouragement and practical suggestions for couples sharing the same space 24/7. They remind us that our spouse can't read our mind, respecting and easing the other's workload is a gift we can offer each other, and togetherness means more than our bodies being in close proximity. As someone who lives full-time aboard a sailboat with my hubby who works from home, I found this book incredibly insightful."

Grace Fox, codirector of International Messengers Canada, and author of *Finding Hope in Crisis*

"It's a rare book whose title makes you grin and whose content keeps you nodding in recognition on almost every page. *Spouse in the House* is the gift I want to give every couple trying to maintain a healthy relationship while navigating the uncertain terrain of two people coexisting in the same space. With wit and wisdom, Ruchti and Melby share insights from their own experience along with practical guidance on finances, communication, and a host of other issues confronting those who bump up against their spouse every loving day."

Maggie Wallem Rowe, author of *This Life We Share*

"I've desperately needed this book for at least five years, since my sweet husband retired . . . and settled down at home. For good. We've both had to pivot to discover new ways to coordinate a homelife that no longer includes four children and two working parents. Thus, I'm absolutely delighted Cynthia Ruchti and Becky Melby have gifted those of us in the HHATT (He's Home All the Time) Club with this perky and practical book. With their wise-friend-next-door tone, the authors cover hard topics with grace and mercy. If you're looking to build greater love and health into your marriage, begin with this fabulous book!"

Lucinda Secrest McDowell, award-winning author of *Soul Strong* and *Life-Giving Choices*

"Yes, I have a spouse in the house—or rather, on our eight-hundred-square-foot live-aboard boat. And during the pandemic, we lived in a three-hundred-square-foot RV so we could care for my ninety-two-year-old in-laws! All I can say is that the wisdom, advice, common sense, and practical help in this book took a very stressful circumstance and transformed it into an opportunity to dance lovingly with each other instead of dancing around each other. Couples can move from being mad to being madly in love again. And Bill, my HHATT (Husband Home All the Time), is equally grateful!"

Pam Farrel, codirector of Love-Wise, and coauthor of the best seller *Men Are Like Waffles, Women Are Like Spaghetti*

SPOUSE
IN THE
HOUSE

Rearranging Our Attitudes to Make
Room for Each Other

Cynthia Ruchti & Becky Melby

KREGEL
PUBLICATIONS

Published in association with the Books & Such Literary Management, 52 Mission Circle, Suite 122, PMB 170, Santa Rosa, CA 95409-5370, www.booksandsuch.com.

All Scripture quotations, unless otherwise indicated, are from the Holy Bible, New International Version®, NIV®. Copyright © 1973, 1978, 1984, 2011 by Biblica, Inc.™ Used by permission of Zondervan. All rights reserved worldwide. www.zondervan.com. The "NIV" and "New International Version" are trademarks registered in the United States Patent and Trademark Office by Biblica, Inc.™

Scripture quotations marked ESV are from the ESV® Bible (The Holy Bible, English Standard Version®), copyright © 2001 by Crossway, a publishing ministry of Good News Publishers. Used by permission. All rights reserved.

Scripture quotations marked NLT are from the Holy Bible, New Living Translation, copyright © 1996, 2004, 2015 by Tyndale House Foundation. Used by permission of Tyndale House Publishers, Inc., Carol Stream, Illinois 60188. All rights reserved.

Scripture quotations marked TLB are from The Living Bible copyright © 1971. Used by permission of Tyndale House Publishers, Carol Stream, Illinois 60188. All rights reserved.

Cataloging-in-Publication Data is available from the Library of Congress.

ISBN 978-0-8254-4678-8, print
ISBN 978-0-8254-7727-0, epub

Printed in the United States of America
21 22 23 24 25 26 27 28 29 30 / 5 4 3 2 1

To Bill.
That ought to cover it, since we both have
a spouse in the house named Bill.

We found and, by God's grace, have kept
good men with good hearts who've agreed to
let us be real in these pages.

Contents

CHAPTER 1

Honey, I'm Home . . . All. The. Time.

— Cynthia —

I'm a member of the HHATT Club. Yes, that's how it's spelled—
He's Home All the Time.

The concept started out as a fictional club. A character in one
of my novels (*Song of Silence*) lost a job she loved and found herself
home all day every day when she'd expected that the best years
of her career were ahead of her. The woman's oh-so-kind-but-a-
teensy-bit-oblivious husband had retired early with the express
purpose of doing nothing with the rest of his life. And he was
skilled at it. (Read further into the book to see how I—I mean,
the character—changed her attitude about his "nothing.")

In the book, a wise counselor suggested the by now depressed
woman should consider joining a book club—the HHATT Club,
specifically. My character followed through, assuming the women
who met in the back room of a quaint coffee shop would discuss,
well, books.

Instead, the self-appointed coordinator said, "We're writing
the book . . . on how to survive when your husband's home all
. . . the . . . time."

The main character felt compelled to say, "I love my husband.
He's a good man."

One of the other members answered, "It's a prerequisite for the HHATT Club. We all love our husbands. We love being with them. It's the 24/7 part that needs a little help."[1]

Like most novelists, I learned a thing or two while writing that book. I got to know the HHATT Club members and their unique, proactive approach to making it work, finding equilibrium amid a sudden overload of togetherness.

The need for equilibrium is perhaps greater than ever. Not since the Industrial Revolution transformed American life from what had been largely agricultural and family-run businesses have we seen such a seismic shift back to two spouses at home. This migration to more time at home can be traced to many factors:

- Advanced degrees can now be earned entirely online.
- A rising entrepreneurial spirit is creating more and more home-run businesses (many with "work-linked" spouses collaborating on the same business, or each running a business of their own).
- Company employees increasingly work remotely to cut down on overhead, commuting a few feet from kitchen to office rather than two hours in sluggish traffic.
- Combine all those realities with as many as ten thousand baby boomers retiring *every day* in the United States.

More and more Americans are finding themselves *not* saying "Have a great day" as both spouses head off to work. Work doesn't necessarily mean leaving the house. They're together more than they expected. And they're unsure what that's supposed to look like relationally. And practically.

When I speak for women's groups and mention the phrase "he's home all the time," I can count on one response reverberating through the audience like a well-timed wave in a football stadium. Each woman lifts her chin a little, then nods knowingly. "Ah. Uh-huh. Yes."

They get it. We get it.

And so do our husbands.

It's not always—okay, it rarely is—a smooth transition when two bodies share the same air. The same remote. The same bathroom. The same standing-room-only spot in the kitchen. We navigated the dance steps without much trouble as newlyweds. Maybe we were delirious.

But now, when more husbands and wives have work-from-home options and are trying to find space for two desks and two office chairs and two business phone calls or online meetings happening concurrently in what was once a spare room . . .

Now, when a deployed spouse is home, but home looks and feels different and the roles they had to abdicate to serve their country aren't easy to reclaim and harder still to relinquish . . .

Now, when retirement throws wide the door of togetherness but every room in the house feels like it's shrinking . . .

> **Being home together is not a phenomenon we need to learn to embrace for an entire day. It may be for the rest of our breaths.**

The interesting thing about 24/7 is that a minute past the "24" part is a brand-new 24/7 with no blank space between. So being home together is not a phenomenon we need to learn to embrace for an entire day. It may be for the rest of our breaths.

And it may be a forced togetherness brought on by illness or impairment, which is already stressful. Or a layoff. Or a company-wide pivot to use remote workers only. Or a worldwide pandemic.

Wow, that sounds melodramatic, doesn't it? If only we were exaggerating. The book in your hands was contracted long before *pandemic* became a household word. For every single household.

Some of these chapters were written in the early months of its raging. Talk about live-in research.

We can whine about the inconvenience of having a spouse in the house more than we think normal, grumble about not having the elbow room we long for, and complain to the person who is experiencing the same thing from the other side of the breakfast bar. Or we can figure out how to survive, discover what our friends are doing to manage their reasons for too much togetherness, and—in our case—put it in a book.

Spouse in the House shares tips and tools we've gathered, insights we often return to for this lifelong learning curve. We *can* move from uncertainty, confusion, or claustrophobia to peace and relationship vitality when both spouses are in the house—whether due to retirement, job loss, caregiving, deployment and reentry, building a business at home, working remotely, or juggling the "they're here, they're gone" of a spouse whose job necessitates long stretches away followed by long stretches at home.

Can we coexist without co-exhausting?

Thriving through the togetherness involves learning new dance moves that will keep us from tripping over each other when we're "gifted" with a 24/7 partner who is dancing to some other tune.

— **Becky** —

It was 1980. A Friday afternoon in November. My husband (who, for the sake of clarity, I'm calling Dr. Snuggles) arrived home from work with a pink slip in hand. He'd been laid off. My first thought was that we needed to give up the idea of trying for a third child. But Dr. Snuggles (yes, I will explain this nickname in a future chapter, and, yes, I have his tepidly enthusiastic permission to use it) assured me it would only be a short layoff.

Right.

Fast-forward eight months. I waddled through the living room, stepping around toys littered by our two sons, full laundry basket propped on what had once been distinguishable as a hip bone. Where was my husband? Sitting on the couch. Why was I the one doing all the work? Couldn't he see my swollen feet, my protruding belly obscuring the laundry-basket hip?

I know what you're thinking. *What a louse. He hadn't budged off that couch or lifted a finger to help her for eight months. The poor beached-whale-looking woman was doing all the cooking, cleaning, and laundry while he just sat there staring at the TV, oblivious to the mess. Not fair!*

But maybe that's not the whole picture. In reality, Dr. Snuggles had taken on several temporary jobs and enrolled in night classes while waiting to get called back to work. On top of that, he had been working full-time and going to school part-time for the prior eight years while I, on the other hand, had worked for two years and then had the luxury of staying home with our children for the next six. Not that the stay-at-home-mom job is a luxury, but for me the option of staying home is.

Looking back on that year, why is that laundry basket versus couch moment the memory that floats to the top? Why don't I remember the times we made meals or cared for the kids together? Why don't I instantly think of how wonderful it was that the four and a half of us could spend extra time together, or that I had a man around who would take over so I could rest my swollen feet and take a nap, a guy who loved me enough to get down on his knees to help me put on my shoes?

Fast-forward to 2017. Our four sons had left the nest and blessed us with four daughters-in-love and fifteen grandchildren. My husband had a successful chiropractic clinic—a career change that was a direct result of the layoff I had whined about. I was working on my eighteenth novel. Life was good. And then . . .

Together we decided it was time for him to enter semi-retirement. We talked about it, thought we were both prepared. We had a good relationship. What could go wrong?

I moved my work space to a desk in one of our spare bed-rooms. I used to have all day and the whole house to myself, alternating between the kitchen table, couch, and standing at a counter with my laptop. But this new arrangement would work, wouldn't it? I had a beautiful view from the window of my spring-green-walled room. If I worked smart, I could reach my daily word count in only two hours a day, six days a week. We would talk about our schedules every evening. We could do this.

And then came the day I was sitting at my desk, finally getting my thoughts in order to begin writing, when I was suddenly aware of a presence in the doorway. Dr. Snuggles stood there, patiently waiting for me to look up. When I did, he said, "Breakfast with the guys got canceled so I'm home all morning."

My fingernails curled into my palms. The cords in my neck tightened. I attempted a calming breath and failed. To my credit, I simply nodded. And waited until the words had fully formed in my head. Then I let him have it.

"I don't think you understand. Do you realize *my* job descrip-tion hasn't changed one bit? I'm not retired! Everything I used to do in nine hours a day I now have to find a way to squeeze into teensy blocks so I have time for you. I have to get my writ-ing done. I can't drop what I'm doing just because you're free." (Notice the overuse of the singular first-person pronoun.)

As I vented, my hubby's face morphed from shock to hurt to anger. It didn't dawn on me until much later the man was simply communicating that his plans had changed. He wasn't actually asking anything of me. That was the moment I knew I was not prepared for 24/7 togetherness. That was the moment I knew I needed help.

For months, Cynthia and I joked about writing this book. I

remember saying, "Couples go to premarital counseling before saying 'I do.' Why doesn't somebody create preretirement counseling so we're ready to say, 'I still do. All. The. Time'?"

When Cynthia came up with our title—*Spouse in the House*—I wrote it as an acronym in an email. SITH. As in Sith lords, those Star Wars antagonists drawing their power from the dark side of the Force, bent on carrying out their evil agendas of domination over their rivals.

The comparison between the spouses in our houses and these Machiavellian warlords made me laugh and wince at the same time. Though exaggerated, there are some parallels to the way I was looking at my very own SITH. And therein lies a key: *the way I was looking at my spouse*. I'm embarrassed to admit it was a light bulb moment when I realized my husband was not the enemy. He is not the antagonist in our life story. He is not my rival. He is not attempting to gain power and dominion over my life or our home.

True, we had things to talk about and work through, but the biggest conflict was in my head, in my idea that our home was *my* domain and *my* time should be my own. It's an ongoing journey, but simply realizing we are on the same team has turned me from a defensive complainer into a woman who is (mostly) thoroughly enjoying more time with her husband, the flexibility and freedom of retirement, and the renewed intimacy this freedom can bring. (BTW, my phone decided that *renewed* should be spelled "re-nude," which gave me the idea to address this topic later in the book.)

> The biggest conflict was in my head, in my idea that our home was *my* domain and *my* time should be my own.

I look forward to sharing my foibles and misconceptions with you as we learn together, with God's help, how to embrace sharing living space (and mental space) with our SITHs.

CHAPTER 2

Love Keeps No Record of Who Cleaned the Toilet Last

— Becky —

What do you do when a system that worked for forty-five years suddenly . . . doesn't?

I was raised in the fifties and sixties by parents whose roles were defined by gender. Dad worked in an office; Mom stayed home and took care of my brother and me, cooked, cleaned, shopped, and ironed my dad's shirts, handkerchiefs, and boxer shorts.

I am not my mother. I do not iron boxer shorts. Still, for more than four decades Dr. Snuggles and I had a plan for who did what when that divided pretty evenly along gender lines. Even during the seasons when I worked in or out of the home, I handled the same stuff my mother did, and Dr. Snuggles took care of the yard, the cars, home repairs, and paying the bills.

And then retirement hit. I know, that makes it sound like an unexpected tidal wave slamming down on us. It wasn't that we hadn't talked and talked and talked about it. But it wasn't until he was actually home (All. The. Time.) that the reality of the change to my life hit like a massive storm surge. How was I going to squish all the things I'd filled my days with into far fewer lines on my planner so I could enjoy my hubby's freed-up time?

You're probably yelling the answer. I know, I know. *Make him help!*

I was fortunate to marry a man who was a good cook. Before we had children, we split the cooking duties, or we cooked together. Once our children came along and my husband's work responsibilities escalated, I took over the culinary role and trained our sons to help. The men always carried the Master of the BBQ role and as each son married, he was given a new gas BBQ grill and the rehearsal dinner was created on the new grill. Now that the kids have launched and we both work from home, we revert back to sharing the cooking (one cooks and the other cleans up) or we both cook.

—Pam Farrel, author of *Red-Hot Monogamy*

Again, I am not my mother. But her voice is still in my head. She taught, by words and example (tapping into what was more pop culture than scripturally sound), how to serve a man, how to never ask for anything, how to be (or at least tell yourself you are) content in any circumstance. My mother would never, ever have made a honey-do list.

So for the first few days of my husband's retirement, I continued on as before, trying to work a little faster and more efficiently. And then came the day . . .

We'd invited friends for dinner. I'd spent the day alternating between cleaning, cooking, and writing. Now it was crunch time. I had less than an hour to put the finishing touches on dinner, set the table, change clothes, do my hair, and put on makeup. I'm embarrassed to say that, looking back, I have no recollection of what Dr. Snuggles had done all day. Maybe he'd been working in the yard. What I do remember is where he was at the moment my internal pressure gauge registered *overwhelmed.*

In. His. Recliner.

Couldn't he see what needed to be done?

I couldn't stomp quite as thunderously then as I had when I was eight months pregnant. In fact, I was doing my best to keep it all bottled up inside and tightly corked . . . except for the occasional slam of a potlid.

And then, just as the cork started to wiggle free, my man walked into the kitchen and said the six most magical words in the English language. No, not "You are beautiful. I love you." He said, "What can I do to help?"

I had a couple of options here. I could have said, "Fine timing, buddy. Look around. It's almost all done already." I could have laser-glared. But I made a choice. I threw my arms around him, kissed him soundly, and then, with a little eye batting and without my go-to snarkiness, told him what still needed to be accomplished.

Corny? Yes. But grace and humor cover a multitude of missed cues. That one little question was a turning point for us. For me, it was accepting, once again, that my man can't read my mind. How is he to know that (in my opinion) there are things that need to be done if I don't verbalize it? We don't always get this right, but we've started taking time most nights to talk about the next day. "What do you have scheduled?" "What do we want to do for fun?" "What do we need to get done first?" And then we ask each other those six magical words: "What can I do to help?"

> Grace and humor cover a multitude of missed cues.

The key to making a division of labor work is to make it work for *you*. There isn't just one right way. But there is one destined-to-fail system: the fifty-fifty method.

Working together to create a master list of everything that needs to be done inside and outside and then categorizing and prioritizing tasks as daily, weekly, and monthly is a great place to start. But treating each item on that list like a playing card—one for you, one for me, one for you, one for me—is a setup for future frustration.

Getting along well requires recognizing that we have different expectations in many situations. Depending on the guests we've invited, I may think the state of the yard and their first impression as they drive up to the house is more important than having the house spotlessly clean. So I'm out there working on that (maybe even obsessing over that) while Becky's inside, wondering why I'm not helping her finish up what she feels is critical but impossible to get done alone.

The point is, who gets to decide what is most important? I'm sure there is a minimum level we can agree on for both the inside and the outside of the house, and we need to help with, or at least allow the other to focus on, that minimum. Beyond that, we need to honor each other's preferences and not expect our spouses to sacrifice what they honestly believe is important so they can help us with what we think is more important. My perceived needs and preferences are not more right or important than hers, and neither are hers more right or important than mine.

—Dr. Snuggles

Inevitably, some days everything on your list is crossed off, but he hasn't touched his. The trash is overflowing, the kids' noseprints are still smeared on the front window, and the toothpaste dabs in the sink have petrified. But when you've spent the day meeting a work deadline, tending to a sick child, or supporting a friend in her marriage crisis, the last thing you need is your spouse jabbing his finger at *your* side of the list.

Built into the fifty-fifty method is the assumption that absolute fairness is achievable. And to make it happen, we must oversee each other. Trouble in the making. There's an adage that fits here: I'm only the boss of *me*.

> For ten years I was my husband's office secretary and para-legal. I have to remind him every now and then that I am not his secretary anymore. Each of us has our own business. I don't feed his cattle. He doesn't write my books.
>
> —Maxine R.

Another approach to the who-does-what-when question is to talk about likes, dislikes, strengths, and weaknesses. Maybe you can't stomach even looking at the brown goo on the bottom of the crisper drawer while he's got guts of titanium. Nothing makes him gag, and cleaning out the fridge is an adventure of discovery. Or he's tried his hand at gardening, but he loses interest when it's time to weed. You love sinking your fingers into the dirt and yanking out those invaders. Embrace and maximize your preferences.

When it comes to a job neither of you enjoy, consider doing it together: one of you fills a trash bag with fossilized French fries from the floor of the van and scrapes dehydrated grape juice out of the cup holders while the other vacuums.

Doing it together works for a lot of daily chores. The math is magical. Two people putting clean sheets on a bed takes far less than half the time of one person doing it alone. If you're emptying the dishwasher while he's scrambling eggs and frying bacon, you're constantly bumping elbows, but what if you decide nudging each other can be fun instead of annoying? What if we use the close quarters to chat and fit in a little playful snuggle time, as Dr. Kevin Leman proposed in his book by that title, *Sex Begins in the Kitchen*?

Just sayin'.

I'd like to tag a footnote onto the comments Dr. Snuggles

made earlier about expectations. One day he finished loading the dishwasher and announced, "The dinner plates should go here in the back instead of the front. See? This way, they don't slide around when you pull out the rack."

Did you know that "retired husband syndrome" is a thing? It's a stress response that affects women globally when their spouse stops working at his job or career. Italian researchers Marco Bertoni and Giorgio Brunello report that almost half the women they studied whose husbands had recently retired experienced escalating stress levels, depression, and insomnia, among other issues.[1] The perception is that a man in the house who no longer is employed and has yet to discover a healthy rhythm of recreation and meaningful activity creates a nightmarish scenario for the entire household. Retired husband syndrome. You weren't imagining things.

—Becky

I've been loading dishwashers for decades. *Who is he to think—?* But then I stopped my internal rant and decided to give it a try. Guess what? He's right. For decades I'd put up with plates rolling out of place. Who knew there was a simple answer?

Lesson learned: it's *our* dishwasher. Not mine. And that same earth-shattering truth applies to the whole place. If he wants to rearrange the spice cabinet, fold bath towels in thirds instead of fourths, or roast the cauliflower instead of steaming it, I need to stop and ask myself if he's actually doing it wrong or simply not doing it my way.

— Cynthia —

Division of labor, huh? We're supposed to divide it? I do not think my husband got that memo. Or if he did, it was written in a language he has not yet studied. He's fluent in English. Pretty fluent. That's it.

"I have called this meeting to order to—"

My husband (who hereafter will be known as Wonderhubby for reasons I'll explain later, but mostly because both Becky and I married men named Bill) squirmed. "Are you firing me?"

"No!" Awkward pause. "Wait. I can do that? No, of course not. But we need to talk."

"I'm always eager to have a serious discussion with you, my love. Especially if it involves me changing something I'm doing. Bring it on."

Okay, I made up that last line.

Let's just pretend he said, "Go on."

"How long was it, my beloved, before you let on that one of your assignments at your job entailed cleaning toilets? How long before you let on that you knew how to perform that task?"

"A while."

I tilted my head coyly to the side.

"Twenty-seven years," he said.

We did have a discussion close to this one, but it started with our working to figure out how to balance the load a little more evenly when company is on its way, much like Becky's initiation into this concept.

He long ago defaulted the kitchen to me, although I personally think it's important to learn how to fend for yourself in the kitchen should KFC and Burger King ever close their doors. But because there's so much last-minute kitchen detail when we're expecting company or extended family, we both knew I needed help.

I drew up a list of the 105 last-minute tasks and offered him the "opportunity" to pick the ones he found least offensive. We established a new tradition. Without my needing to ask, he now takes it upon himself to vacuum the carpeting and clean the toilets. That leaves me with a manageable 103 last-minute tasks. Success!

And it turns out, now that he's home all the time, I can tap into his desire for efficiency if he needs to go to town. He doesn't mind stopping at the grocery store, as long as each grocery item is clearly spelled out on the list. What spurs him on is his love of a bargain. His eyes light up when he can report that he saved twenty-three cents on spaghetti noodles and got two boxes of cereal for the price of one.

And I celebrate with him.

But there's no denying we have yet to master the dance steps that will make us feel the workload is evenly distributed. The unfortunate truth is that home chores never retire. But how they're divided may need to change.

Even distribution is not the goal, though, as Becky said. It's unattainable and fluctuates with our individual calendars, health issues, interests, and skills. The true goal is to manage expectations when two spouses share the same space but not necessarily the same work schedules.

For us, surprise attacks spell certain doom. If he asks, unannounced, if I can help him for "a few minutes" with the project he's working on in the garage, I adjust my expectations by assuming it will be a few minutes to the tenth power. And he adjusts his expectations by knowing I need a heads-up. If I'm aware of it ahead of time, I can do my best to shuffle some must-dos so I can be available for his "Would you please . . . ?"

Home all the time isn't the same thing as *free all the time*. For either spouse. Respecting and easing the other's workload is a gift we can offer each other.

Home all the time isn't the same thing as *free all the time*. For either spouse. Respecting and easing the other's workload is a gift we can offer each other.

In few instances will your workload balance itself naturally.

For most of us, we'll have to have a sit-down talk. The goal can't be even-Steven or someone will always be disappointed. But imagine how the atmosphere in the home changes when we ask each other, "What can I do to help shoulder your burden today?"

Sounds familiar, doesn't it?

You may recall something similar from the Bible when the apostle Paul said this: "Bear one another's burdens, and so fulfill the law of Christ" (Galatians 6:2 ESV).

At one time, I didn't think that verse of Scripture applied to husbands and wives, since Paul was addressing brothers and sisters in Christ in a church context. Then it struck me. He may be my husband, but he's also my brother in Christ. On days when the burden bearing seems one-sided, remembering that "he ain't heavy, he's my brother" helps me realign my thoughts like a dance student aligning her feet with the footprints painted on the studio floor.

Love empowers us to bear each other's burdens, and not only carry each other's troubles but carry out God's design.

There it is again. That word that changes everything—*love.*

As a preteen with stars in my eyes, I saw that tall, dark sixth grade guy with the soft gray eyes as a superhero. I married him eight years later, reaching out to tug on the hem of his superhero cape to make sure it was still intact. But the cape needed washing and ironing and lost a little of its gleam in the dusty atmosphere of life.

One day, it struck me that a man who is faithful, who stays, who loves and sacrifices and for a while made pancakes for every meal because my morning sickness couldn't tolerate the smell of anything else is the best kind of superhero.

Leaps tall buildings? No. But he loves me well. Hence, Wonderhubby.

I use the nickname a lot on social media. When people meet my Bill, they often say, "Oh! Is this Wonderhubby?" Embarrassing for him the first time. Now, it's the nickname he chose when I offered him several options for this book so readers can tell if it's my Bill or Becky's Bill we're talking about. (The other options were a lot more embarrassing.)

—Cynthia

Though my Bill is and will always be my hero, his nickname is not quite as superheroish as Wonderhubby's. Sometime in our first years of marriage we started using gag-worthy cutesy names on Christmas gift tags. Neither of us can remember when or why, but he became Snuggles and I was Cuddles. Years later, after he earned his doctor of chiropractic degree, I discovered a children's TV show created in the UK called *Doctor Snuggles*, so I upgraded his nickname. I don't often call him that in real life, but now that the name is public, all of our friends are using it. You're welcome, honey.

—Becky

CHAPTER 3

The Line Down the Middle

— Cynthia —

Some women say a husband perpetually in the house can feel like an invasion—of her schedule, privacy, space, mental space, domain. But isn't it supposed to feel like home for *both* marriage partners?

Social media feeds sizzled with nonmedical fallout of a shelter-in-place order during the global crisis that emerged on the world stage in early 2020. Though many posts referred to the horrific toll the pandemic was taking on individuals and families suffering from the disease and its fallout, a number of posts cried out, "Help me! I'm trapped in my own home with *those* people."

The *those* were for the most part kids, siblings, or spouses, linked by love yet divided by what they perceived as too much togetherness.

Parents out of work, kids whose schools had closed down, college students sent home from their dorms . . .

In some homes, a mix of all three scenarios made for tensions that ran high and felt nothing like a "let's all pile into the family room for an unknown length of time" adventure. Add to that a palpable global concern, crippling uncertainty, and financial threats.

A perfect setup for human collisions.

Jerry Seinfeld created a comedy routine out of scenarios with a "close talker," someone who stood just a tad too close, perpetually violating an invisible but scientifically documented circle of socially acceptable space we—in particular, Americans—have come to depend on.

How close is too close? Intimate conversations take place with a separation of about eighteen inches, psychological research tells us. Casual conversations are comfortable for most people in a range between two feet and four feet. Impersonal communication takes place beyond four feet.

So a new acquaintance who stands a foot away in a face-to-face conversation sets off internal alarms. Even a friend who tells about her day while standing less than two feet away feels like an invader to a human's invisible personal-space boundary.

Even when love creates the relationship, skipping deodorant still causes an issue.

High-anxiety people need an even wider circle than those standards.

Some space situations—both spouses at home all the time, kids and parents home all the time, or too many people in too little square footage—feel like an overcrowded elevator. Few people *don't* squirm if pressed into a confined space like that. Where do I look? How do I breathe? Who had garlic for lunch? Someone in this elevator doesn't believe in deodorant.

Even when love creates the relationship, skipping deodorant still causes an issue.

A family in our neighborhood dealt with a space issue for many years after moving into an American foursquare farmhouse with a chimney that, for heat purposes, ran from the basement through the first floor, second floor, attic, and above the roofline—right through the center of the house.

The chimney's presence was most disruptive for the modern family living in the home. On the first floor, it squeezed the main pathway from the kitchen to the rest of the house into what qualifies as intimate space. It shrank the landing at the base of the stairs. It formed a roadblock for a person moving from any of the first-floor rooms to any other, or to the second-floor bedrooms.

Despite the inconvenience, the family lived with a not-even-close-to-code eighteen inches between the chimney and the stairs—as in eighteen inches of main passageway between the kitchen and everything else. The fallout was multiple traffic jams every single day.

Extended family gathered in the kitchen, as many families do, creating more complex jams during holidays. The buffet line from the kitchen counter to the dining room necessitated one-way traffic only. All the time. So did simply going to the kitchen sink for a drink of water.

The homeowners talked often about how much more complicated it became when either husband or wife or a guest was on crutches or using a walker or recuperating from a whatever-you-do-don't-twist-sideways back injury. Can you imagine?

I can.

It's my house.

It's been awkward for forty-plus years. We've known for a long time that a to-code, reasonable walkway is thirty-six inches minimum. *Minimum.* But it wasn't until I connected our narrow passageway with the concept of invasion of personal space that I realized, *No wonder it feels worse than just the minor inconvenience of needing to travel single file in our home, the need to use vocal* beep beep beep*s when backing up!*

Don't even ask how we moved furniture, hauled mattresses, wiggled major appliances, and carried suitcases through that space.

On the other hand, it was a great spot to hang mistletoe. There was no escape.

The inconvenience of it all took a positive turn when my husband started saying, "Excuse me, my love," if we both needed that eighteen inches at the same time. Adding two words—"my love," a term of endearment, to "excuse me," a common courtesy—changed the constant traffic jams into something we could live with a little longer. It turned our attention from the space itself to the relationship between those inhabiting the space.

After all, togetherness isn't merely being together. Our bodies may be in close proximity to each other. Are our hearts? Our attentions? Our affections?

We're in construction mode right now . . . and have been for six months as of this writing. Replacing our furnace meant that our heating system no longer requires a chimney. So it came down, brick by brick, from above the roofline, through the attic, the second floor, the first floor, and the basement.

I won't go into the apocalyptic mess that made, which greeted me after I returned from a long speaking-engagement trip.

According to the spouse in my house, he'd already spent time on cleanup. Who am I to complain or doubt his definition of *thorough*? The chimney's gone. And that open hole in the floor where it used to be? He was willing to temporarily patch that a day or two later, saving me from falling into the basement as I descended the stairs in the morning.

The point?

Big problems can sometimes be tempered by small acts of courtesy.

When my guy started adding "my love" to his "excuse me" during the plethora of times we both needed the same space, the eighteen inches of room grew even more intimate. In a good way. How easy would it be to add common courtesy and an endearment when speaking to our SITH?

— Becky —

"Stay on your side!"

I was seven. My brother was five. Back before kids' car seats and seat belts, personal space in the car was dictated by the number of people in the family. Though I didn't appreciate it at the time, having only one sibling was a huge blessing that gave me title to half of the red vinyl in the back seat of our 1959 Plymouth Fury. I didn't appreciate it because every once in a while, the toe of my brother's Red Ball Jets or a crayon that had half melted in the back window would trespass into my territory. Ew! Boy cooties!

Sixty years later, I should be way beyond this pettiness. I *should* be. But when Dr. Snuggles assembled his model train set in the middle of the living room floor—and left it there for more than a week—it was all I could do to keep from yelling, "Stay on your side!"

If he's watching a shoot-'em-up movie and *Pow! Zap! Bang!* interrupts my every thought, is it okay to scream, "Take your boy cooties to the basement"?

As the only girl in our family, I had my own room, and everything in it had an invisible label: *mine*. I never had to share clothes, dolls, vinyl records, or breathing room. I didn't have to share my friends. If I was hosting a slumber party and my brother wandered into girl territory, I handled it swiftly with one word: "Mooooooom!"

As a teen, I could unplug the princess phone from the jack in my parents' bedroom and bring it into my room, where I'd hide under the covers and pour my heart out to a friend.

After high school, I lived at home and attended a local commuter college until I got married and moved into a twelve-by-sixty-foot mobile home with my husband and, much to his surprise, my twelve-year-old golden retriever. Three bodies sharing 720 square feet—before tiny houses were trendy.

I remember sitting outside on the concrete steps sometime

during our first year of marriage, writing in my journal, tears streaming down my face. We'd had a tiff and I didn't know where to go with my emotions. I couldn't call a friend—our only phone sat on an end table next to his recliner. My bedroom was his bedroom—I couldn't yell for Mom to tell him to leave or hang a "no boys allowed" sign and slam the door.

That journal I held in my hands as I sat on the step proved to be a lifesaver. Even if I was sitting a few feet away from my husband, I could crawl into my own little therapy session via pen and paper. I could vent until my hurt or frustration was spent and give rein to some creativity in the process. A poem from back then:

> On our down days,
> being alone with you
> can be awkward,
> cold, and uncomfortable . . .
> Unless I'm wrapped
> in the warmth
> of my own thoughts.
> I find it easy
> to lose myself
> in blueprints of insignificance
> when I'm trying to shut you out.

Go ahead, laugh. I share this not only to prove I was a pretty lame poet in my melodramatic twenties but to give inspiration. Put it on paper. Get it out. Don't worry how it sounds. It's amazing how cathartic it can be.

Living well together in tight quarters leaves no room for building walls. Focus on building friendship instead.
—Grace Fox, sailboat dweller and author of *Moving from Fear to Freedom: A Woman's Guide to Peace in Every Situation*

Even in cramped quarters, there are a lot of ways to create personal space:

- Walk out your front door, imagine you are your spouse, and walk back in. How do you feel? At home . . . or like a visitor? Are there comfortable places for you to relax, work, create? What about the decor? Does it express your tastes or is it a little too spouse-specific? (I will confess right here that back in the nineties, while sharing space with five males of various ages, I painted my kitchen pink and accented with flowered wallpaper. In my defense, it was the only nod to femininity in a house filled with sweaty socks, pet rats, and BB guns.)
- In a spirit of cooperation (unlike when I drew an imaginary line down the middle of the back seat), collaborate on defining separate work or hobby spaces by changing furniture groupings or multipurposing living areas (desk by day, coffee table by night).
- Define work hours and communicate about needed time and space. One friend carried a basket of dirty laundry past her husband's basement office space, filled the washer, and walked out with a load of clean laundry . . . only to find out later she'd had a walk-on role in her hubby's important video conference. Create signs—literal or otherwise—to let your spouse know when you're "on air."

My husband's office space is in our sunroom, which opens to our kitchen and family room. Our house is completely open concept, so there is no separate living space to shut a door other than bedrooms and bathrooms.

On Friday afternoons, he often has video conference calls. There have been times when I've run out to get a carload of groceries and arrived home to discover he's on an active call. Imagine carrying in loud plastic grocery bags with your spouse on a video conference six feet away. I've found myself tiptoeing around, trying to get meat and cheese out of bags and into the refrigerator as quietly as possible, trying to stay out of the camera angle, all while feeling guilty for royally disrupting his workday.

—Sarah Forgrave, author of *Prayers for Hope and Healing*

- Be flexible. Striving to make the most out of a less-than-ideal situation can be an adventure, if you choose to look at it that way. In our first house—a two-bedroom, one-bath Cape Cod—I had a desk with a manual typewriter in our poorly insulated, unfinished, freezing-in-the-winter-and-sweltering-in-the-summer attic. I shared the space with mice and spiders, but it was *mine*. While I dreamed of the day I'd have my own comfy work space, I found a way to create a solution that worked. Today we are empty nesters sharing a four-bedroom house which provides plenty of work space for both of us. But flexibility and a sense of adventure are still required. You see, we also spend weeks at a time in a twenty-six-foot camper. Two bodies sharing 260 square feet . . .

We don't necessarily need to rearrange furniture to make room for each other. Sometimes we need to rearrange our attitudes and reactions.

While the layout and atmosphere of your house matters, I've also slowly realized since my husband retired that we don't necessarily need to rearrange furniture to make room for each other. Sometimes we need to rearrange our attitudes and reactions. Creating mental space can counteract a lack of square feet labeled *mine.*

Here are some tips I've found helpful for making room in your head for the person you share your home with:

- *Pray.* Dump it all out. God is big enough to take it . . . and to give you the grace to change your perspective. Years after I was journaling in our first home together, I discovered the healing therapy of keeping a prayer journal where I pour out my heart to God and record His answers. Often just the writing is enough to change the situation or my attitude toward it. Rereading my own words lets me see where pride and selfishness have weaseled their way in and gives me the breathing room I need to work up the courage to apologize or talk it out. Journaling your prayers also allows you to look back and celebrate the skills you've learned while adapting to a new way of thinking.
- *Leave.* No, not permanently. Take a drive or a walk or have lunch with a friend—one who will listen and empathize but not feed your dissatisfaction. A friend who will help you see the good in the person you live with is a beautiful gift.
- *Tune in.* Music has the power to lift us above our crowded circumstances and fill us with unexplainable joy. Worship songs, or oldies that remind us of the early days of our relationship, literally change the chemicals bathing our brains.
- *Tune out.* Invest in a box of earplugs—the chunky yellow ones that look like little barrels. I tried three different kinds until I found these marriage-saving miracles of slow-recovering PVC foam. They shut out snoring as well as the evening news if you can't handle what's going on in the world. I'd also recommend a pair of quality earphones

or noise-canceling headphones. During our five weeks of living in 260 square feet last year, audiobooks and podcasts gave us both needed mental space while we shared tight quarters.

- *Serve.* An act of pure love, even when we don't feel like it, can soften our hearts. Make a favorite meal, give a spontaneous foot massage, invite your SITH on a date, do one of his chores. It will likely result in some gratitude and affection coming your way. But even if it doesn't, an act of Jesus love is good for the soul.

Years ago I met a woman who worked second shift while her husband had a third-shift job and slept during the day. "That must be so hard on your marriage," I said. "Oh no," she replied. "That's the only way we can get along!"

Funny, yes. But sadly, many couples haven't found constructive ways to make being together work, so drawing a line down the middle to separate them seems like the best option. Cynthia and I hope our suggestions can be springboards for you and your spouse to find ways of erasing the dividing lines while still finding healthy personal space. And remember, we may be past the age of yelling "Moooooooom!" when things don't go our way, but we have a heavenly Father just waiting to answer when we cry "Daaaaaaaddy!"

I write books for a living, which means I work from home. You have probably heard of authors who go to coffee shops and whip up amazing stories in the midst of all the noise and distraction of their favorite café. Yeah, that's not me. I need quiet. No music. No interruptions.

Then my hubby retired. He is my favorite person in the whole world, so having him around all the time was something

I looked forward to. Except that my writing room does not have a door.

After six months of his being home, we still haven't fixed that. We have figured out that it is easier (and cheaper) to fix our attitudes than to install a door.

—Tessa Afshar, author and speaker

CHAPTER 4

I Never Used to Be a Night Owl,
but It's the Only Time I Can Be Alone

— Becky —

I had a few moments before getting up to speak at a Christmas luncheon, so I sat down next to a woman I've known for years. The usual "How are you doing?" questions ensued. When I mentioned Dr. Snuggles was about to retire, her hand slid over mine. "Oh . . ."

The look of pure sympathy in her eyes was my first introduction to the He's Home All the Time Club, that group of women Cynthia mentioned in chapter 1 who lift their chin, nod, and say, "Ah. Uh-huh. We get it."

Now that I'm a card-carrying member of this sorority of empathetic women, I'd like to share some of my sisters' stories to let you know that, whether you and your spouse are retired, about to be, or for some other reason are both at home—a lot—you are not alone.

Let's start with the woman who grabbed my hand. "Every time I pick up the car keys," she said, "he's right there. Like a puppy when you jangle a leash. I can't go to the grocery store alone. I can't get my hair done without him tagging along. If I want to have lunch with a friend, I have to find tactful ways of telling him he's not invited."

Here are some of the other women in this club, with their own stories to tell.

Kiley

Kiley and her husband have been married fourteen years. She was a software tester when they first married. Today she home-schools their three children and runs a small online resale shop. At the time I asked for her thoughts on 24/7 togetherness, her husband was on month nine of working at home full-time. After years of commuting, they are grateful for the commute he takes now—from their bed to the desk chair in their bedroom.

Kiley says, "We often compare our life to pioneer times when Ma would ring the supper bell and Pa would come in from the field for lunch and a kiss, then head back to work. For us it feels right. We are blissfully happy."

When they first switched to that life-work style, they had a few bumps, she readily admits. "I was always the manager of all things house and kid related. If someone needed a dentist appointment, I made it and saw to it that the attendee arrived on time with freshly brushed teeth. I was happy being the 'chief house coordinator.' But now that we are a consta-family, life (and appointment making) is different. We must all be in each other's business 24/7. If someone in the house sneezes, we are guaranteed four resounding gesundheits."

When presented with the need to attend physical therapy three times a week, Kiley polished her chief house coordinator badge and got to coordinating. She could disrupt her husband's working hours the least by getting the kids started on their school-work, telling him she would be back shortly, and heading to her appointment. Easy.

Too easy.

Then came the day her husband had planned to be gone at the same time she was set to leave. Chaos ensued as she quickly arranged a last-minute grandma visit. Appointment: made. Husband's plans: unscathed. Crisis averted.

Wrong.

"It happened," she says. "The calendar 'discussion' . . . and I use that word lightly. My husband, the man I love and adore, made *my* online cloud calendar viewable to *him*. He now knew the time of every dentist and doctor appointment, playdate, birthday, and event. I was in shock. I was angry. I was hurt. I had nothing particularly interesting on my calendar, and certainly nothing to hide. But for fourteen years I had managed it all, and here he was trying to take over. After all, what is a mother's purpose in life if not to be coordinator of all things? We 'discussed.' And 'discussed.' And 'discussed.'"

For about a week after their "discussion," Kiley says she passive-aggressively added her husband to every appointment, practice, and outing. She clogged his work calendar with Cinco de Mayo and Groundhog Day reminders. If he wanted to know what he was missing, he was about to find out!

Sandy

Sandy and I have been friends for more than forty years, through all the bumps and bruises of raising kids and all the roller-coaster stages of marriage. Her wise words have pulled me out of some "Did I really marry the right guy?" moments. Sandy loves her husband dearly. But when he retired . . .

"We've had our vacation home for years," she says. "He's always loved taking off by himself or with one of our boys for hunting or fishing weekends. Now, when he's got all the time in the world, he can't go without me? What? He says he realizes he hasn't always been there for me over the years, so he wants to make it up to me. He wants us to be together more. But he's retired. What does 'more' than 24/7 even look like? I feel blindsided. I know his intentions are good, but I'm being smothered here. How do I say, 'You're driving me crazy!' without hurting his feelings?"

Nancy

Newly married to her second husband when I first met her, Nancy had spent forty-two years as a stay-at-home, homeschooling mom before her first husband died. I asked her about the problems unique to being home-together-all-the-time newlyweds in their sixties.

"John was already retired when we met. A second marriage, especially later in life, doesn't have the history of patterns and responses that long marriages have. One of the things I've struggled with is getting used to having someone watching over me while I'm working on projects or regular home maintenance. Being watched closely can feel suffocating at times. Even though I know his watchfulness is really concern that I don't overwork or stress myself physically, it's still hard."

HHATT Club Sisters' Solutions

Kiley says, "After I realized my husband wasn't taking the passive-aggressive bait, we had something that much more closely resembled a discussion in the traditional sense. The immediate solution was to once again make *my* calendar solely viewable to *me*.

"I still don't quite understand why it bothered me that he had access to my calendar. He was far too busy to want to coordinate the mundane aspects of our lives. Making the family calendar mine again did make me feel like I wasn't in danger of losing the person I have identified as for so many years. I knew at the time I wasn't being logical. I'm just thankful my husband allowed grace to replace his annoyance."

What does Kiley do now? She adds him to any important appointments that take place during his workday but leaves the everyday appointments and events to her calendar. "God may have designated him the head of the household, but he happily handed the chief house coordinator assignment off to me. After all, my husband knows I'll give him a heads-up when Groundhog Day is nearing. Until our next 'discussion,' we are back to being blissfully happy."

Sandy and her husband sought counseling. In that safe environment, with a trusted mediator to guide them, she was able to say, "You're driving me crazy!"

The outcome?

"I realized we wanted the same thing in our marriage—loving each other," Sandy says. "I also admitted I needed to change some things about my attitude and perspective. After reflection and listening to the Lord, I'm more comfortable sharing my space, my time, my movies and TV shows. (He's watching HGTV with me now!)"

After a lot of talking . . . and then more talking . . . Sandy and her husband have come to a place where she can tell him she wants to take a walk alone and he's okay with that. She credits professional counseling for helping them navigate rough waters. "I have friends who have lost their husbands too early," she says. "I want us to thoroughly enjoy this time."

> Taking the time to listen and explain things clearly is the key.

In Nancy's words, "Most of our conflicts have been over miscommunication. Taking the time to listen and explain things clearly is the key. Balancing all the together time with some individual activities helps us appreciate the times we're together. My advice to others is, whenever possible, do some of those bucket-list items. Life is short and can change too quickly."

> After forty-eight years of full-time employment, I finally felt released from my sentence. I was retired. I walked through the front door with the feeling that, at long last, I could begin to

enjoy the fruits of my labor—only to find it was like trying to merge onto a busy multiple-lane highway. I was, metaphorically, asking Becky to move over and make room for me. I was interposing myself in the middle of her world. It's a lot to ask for her to change her life on a dime and, literally overnight, take a whole new turn. She handled it with a great deal of grace in spite of the shock to her world.

—Dr. Snuggles

(Becky's addendum: Dr. Snuggles is showing a great deal of grace when he says I handled the transition with grace! As previously noted, I did not.)

— Cynthia —

It is a truth universally accepted that how we're individually wired by our Creator both enhances and complicates our relationships. Our differences balance us, supporting what I sometimes say to my husband: "Together, we make one pretty decent human being."

But what's different about the way we're wired—sometimes polarly so—can also make marriage a study in compensating, negotiating, and work-arounds.

Marriage is an ocean journey. No sailor sets a course and successfully navigates the waters without constant, minor course corrections and adjustments to wind, weather, currents, swells, hidden dangers, and unexpected hazards.

If ignored or handled poorly, our differences become a study in frustration.

A key area of potential discontent is the often-ignored-because-we-love-each-other-so-what's-the-problem mismatch of ideas about the question, "How much togetherness is too little, too much, or just right?" Our marriage has traversed seasons when we had to work hard at balancing our need to be together and our need to be alone. Solutions didn't come naturally. They rarely do. And over the years, those needs have shifted for one or both of us:

- *Newlywed haze*—"Baby, baby, baby, I don't ever want you out of my sight or allow any distance between us. Like, if I can't touch you right now, you're too far away. Let's share a sink when we brush our teeth together. We don't need a double bed. The two of us in one sleeping bag sounds like heaven."

- *Baby on the way days*—"Honey, I love you, but can you quit doing that?" "Quit what?" "Breathing. You're rocking the bed and it's making me nauseated."

- *Young children in the house phase*—"Togetherness? What's that? We're in survival mode. We haven't had a date night since . . . before my water broke."

- *Teens plus a toddler in the house craze*—"What are you doing in the master closet, honey? Wait, you have a TV in here? And a coffee maker? Is there room on that love seat for me?"

- *Shift work glaze*—"Good morning." (Brief kiss.) "Thanks. Heading for bed." "I warmed it up for you."

- *Job loss malaise*—"What are you doing?" "Watching you work." "That's creepy. Don't you have something to do outside?" "Did it already."

- *Work from home daze*—"Rough day at work." "Yeah, me too." "You work from home." "Which is rough." "Well, sure. But it's not the same." (Blank stare.)

- *Health concern frays*—"I'm going for a walk, love." "I'll get my coat." "I'm going by myself." "Is that wise?" "I need time to think. Alone."

- *Caregiver maze*—"Where are you going?" "Out to get the mail, hon. I won't be long." "What if I need you?" "I have my cell phone right here. You can text me or call, but you do realize the mailbox is only thirty feet from the house, right?" "Yes, but [pained groan] what if I need you?" *And what if I need you not to need me quite this much?*
- *Another job loss malaise*—"Why don't you call Ralph to go fishing with you? Great day for it." "Don't feel like fishing." "Since when?"
- *Semi-retirement mayonnaise* (admittedly I ran out of words that rhyme with *phase*, but this isn't a bad substitute, since things have to be broken, added, and combined thoroughly [season to taste] to make a good mayo)—"Can't we do something together today?" "Like what?" "Just drive around." "I have a virtual call at ten." "Come on!" "How about at three? I'm free then." "I'm not." "What do you have scheduled? Oh, right. Your nap."
- *Retirement reappraise*—"Nothing's the same now, is it?" "Not one thing." "We're going to have to rethink all of it, aren't we?" "Looks like it." "Want to go out for an ice-cream cone and talk about it?" "My book club meets in twenty minutes. Here. At the house. You might want to put on pants."

I left basketball, baseball, and football seasons off the above list for a reason. As in many—not all—households, my husband and I have vastly different tolerance levels for televised sporting events. I like a football game once a week or so, especially if it's a team I care about. But I'm satisfied to watch no more than the final two minutes of a basketball game. To me, televised basketball games are a continuous flow of crowd noise, repetitive commentary, and squeaky shoes. To me, baseball season is best described as "nothing happening, nothing happening, nothing happening, nothing happening, home run, brief pause, another game the next day."

My husband is extra skilled at finding a ball game to interest him. He tells me I should be grateful he doesn't like hockey. I could consider his obsession an opportunity for "me time." Everyone who shares space all day every day needs individual interests and a breather from one another (yes, even newlyweds). But too often, I've viewed his sports hobby as an intentional distancing on his part. I'm working on shifting my perception on that topic. What if that's his version of alone time? Why would I resent his need for sports space but expect him to respect my need for alone time with a good book, classical music, and tea?

Our personalities, our capacities for the alone-together ratio, and our choices for what counts as a "worthy" relaxation activity will naturally be different and call for compromise.

Marriage has always been a balancing act. And it can change from one day to the next. When my mom died, I craved leaning my face into my husband's chest, melting in the warmth of his strength and the power of his embrace. A week later, I needed quiet time alone to process what had happened. My mom was gone. Part of the emotional journey required me to work through some of it solo.

Author Kathi Lipp proposes, "We're not meant to be with our people 24/7." Note that she's not referring to people in general but "our" people, those closest to us, those we choose, those to whom we've pledged a lifetime of love and respect, faithfulness and devotion.

Without time alone, time together can grow stale.

We all need time to think. Time to work through issues that are between us individually and the God we serve. Time to unwind, regroup, and pursue passions that our spouse either doesn't share or finds just a tick shy of repulsive.

The key to retirement is to talk about it *before* it happens. For people who work outside the home, homelife is weekends. It's not the daily stuff that needs doing, the daily routines that need establishing. I worked at home most of my life. Chuck went to the office all his working life. After he retired, I still needed to write. I still needed to go to my meetings and the gym and the store and all the other things he never saw me do. I needed to explain why I read while eating lunch. I needed to explain not talking when I was at the computer. He needed to tell me his vision of being home. *Before.*

—Gayle Roper, novelist and author of *A Widow's Journey*

Without time alone, time together can grow stale. When we develop and explore life individually, we bring something fresh to the dinner table conversation. When we participate in activities and interests that fill our souls and our storehouse of stories, we offer our partner a more well-rounded experience.

Finding time and space for the non-together moments may be as simple as putting on earbuds or headphones to create virtual distance or, as Becky said, as intentional as designating a reading corner in the sunroom or creating a sports den in the basement, upgrading to a man cave and a she shed, or even finding time for a short solo getaway for each marriage partner.

Without guilt. Without fear that if one or the other needs a moment, it's an unhealthy threat to the relationship. The need for alone time is not gender specific. He needs his time. She needs hers. The degree to which that need manifests itself is individual and unique. But honoring and respecting that very real need may be the healthiest move we can make to keep our marriage vibrant and vital.

CHAPTER 5

To TV or Not to TV? How Can We Manage Relaxation Differences?

— Cynthia —

Televised sports is one of those "be careful what you pray for" conundrums. I learned that the hard way. One winter, our satellite provider deleted Wonderhubby's favorite sports channels because of a negotiation dispute. He had no other option but to watch bass fishing tournament television and reruns of everything we'd seen already. As I said, be careful what you pray for.

As mentioned in the previous chapter, my husband's passion for televised sports is in a whole different league (see what I did there?) from mine. He mongo-enjoys sports. By comparison, I do not.

It's okay.

I wasn't really conscious of *praying* that my SITH would feel compelled to stop watching a steady stream of sports, interspersed with fishing and hunting and survival shows, which probably technically count as sports in their own right.

So imagine my surprise when public safety concerns shut down the sports world just prior to March Madness one winter. Yes, even I, the sports-challenged spouse, know what March Madness is. And not only college basketball, but all sports were brought to a screeching halt that year by global health concerns. All of them.

Wonderhubby spent several days in his recliner with the remote pointed at the blank television screen. What a shock to his system.

The lack of sports entertainment didn't matter more to him than what was going on in the world. He cared far more about keeping us safe and provided for, about protecting me and weathering the uncertainty with us hand in hand, emotionally.

But staying at home more than we already had been held new challenges without my husband's sports-watching hobby.

As many times as we had disagreed about control of the remote, and in particular about baseball-basketball-football-and-all-their-postseasons-overtimes-and-extra-innings, my heart went out to him. To the players. To coaches and owners. And to other fans like the one who lived under the same roof with me.

It wasn't a life lesson for him. (Or if it was, that's his story to tell.) But it was an attitude-adjusting life lesson for me.

I have four sports teams I follow. When one of them is having a good season, I usually follow pretty closely. (Yes, my wife would probably say that means a game is on a lot of the time in our house, although she should have added rounds and matches, since I also appreciate watching golf and tournament tennis.) The Milwaukee Bucks were having their best season in decades the year sports vaporized. Their star player looked like he'd be awarded his second MVP in a row. Then suddenly, in the middle of the season, no more games. No playoffs. No championship. Sports disappeared almost overnight because of global health concerns. It felt like I lost whole teams of vicarious friends.

—Wonderhubby

Oh. Makes more sense now.

—Cynthia

Isn't a job layoff supposed to be cushioned by the home to which the dismissed retreats? In agricultural societies from the beginning of recorded history, home was both haven and workplace. The same is true with many craftsmanship careers. Can it still be both workplace and relaxing haven when a couple works from home or manages a business together from a home office?

Whatever puts a husband and wife in the same space for extended periods of time—or for the rest of our lives—how do we maintain togetherness God applauds without losing the individuality and interests God created within us? How do we create mental and emotional space for pursuing the things that recharge us without creating mental or emotional distance?

What if one of us has a hard time sitting still and the other has grown fond of—or rather, attached to—the remote and his (let's say *his* for the sake of example) recliner?

What if a domicile that had been a quiet, glorious sanctuary for one partner is suddenly thrumming, day and night, with noise from the TV or cacophony-on-its-way-to-music from a spouse who now has time to pursue his interest in guitar, saxophone, piano, drums, bagpipes?

Is camping out in a recliner a legitimate place to relax and vegging out in front of the TV an inalienable right? Is online shopping a recreational activity or a vice? If a spouse finds solace and relaxation making pottery and the other is allergic to clay, is it a "too bad, so sad" situation?

Habits or hobbies can derail into irreconcilable differences. What can we do to keep that from happening?

My mom, often sleep-deprived and tired in ways I couldn't imagine until both of us were older, seemed to resent my dad's attempts to relax, especially when TV was involved. Both of them poured themselves into their respective careers. Mom and Dad loved each other and admired each other's professions. But the

he-can't-possibly-be-as-tired-as-I-am attitude sometimes perme-
ated my childhood home.

Uncomfortable with the tension that created in an otherwise
loving atmosphere, I have a built-in radar that warns me to keep
my expectations in check, and resist resentment-like responses
to my now home-all-the-time husband with a man-shaped divot
in his recliner. Our needs for and means of relaxing don't have
to match. Our energy levels are different because our genetics,
heritage, traditions, and physical bodies
are different by divine design. We spent
our childhoods in the same town, but not
the same home. Our brains, hearts, lungs,
muscles, nervous systems, eyelids, lips,
and toenails are completely different. Why
would we think our leisure time has to be
all matchy-matchy?

**Why would
we think our
leisure time
has to be all
matchy-matchy?**

But if mine interferes with his, or his interferes with my
preferred methods of relaxing, something's gotta give.

Good thing we both like long walks on the beach.

Too bad we live half a state away from the nearest beach, half
a continent away from the nearest ocean.

We can stew in our mismatched methods of chillaxing— Oh!
I promised myself I'd never use that phrase in a book. My kids
and grandkids will never let me live it down!

We can gripe about our differences regarding watching TV
versus reading a book, or a cooking show finale versus a *CSI* rerun,
or cranking up the sound versus the utter joy of absolute quiet.
Or we can find ways to let each other be who we are. And—like
so much relationship problem-solving—it starts with communication and compensating for our differences.

We make a big deal out of watching the shows we both enjoy,
treating them like mini date nights. And we've agreed not to
disparage each other's favorite programs. Sometimes the kindest

thing we can do for one another is say, "I'll watch my show in the other room," or, "I think I'll go read in the sunroom for a while."

> Love can be sharing a favorite TV show or two remotes and two devices and two shows, then a really great discussion of what we each learned—in CliffsNotes form!
> —Pam Farrel, Love-Wise marriage and family author and speaker

I'm asking myself new questions now when his recliner time or viewing options seem like they're standing between us.

- Where am *I* standing? Nearby? Reachable? Accessible?
- Am I willing to adjust around someone else's schedule simply because I love him? It's the stance I gladly took with every child I birthed.
- Is he relaxing or bored? If he's bored, it may be his responsibility to fix that, but is there a way *I* can be what he finds intriguing?
- If I choose to do something else when he chooses yet another rerun or fishing show, will I do it with a sigh or respect his different-from-me ways of relaxing?

We laugh about it now, but my husband once complained about how much screen time our kids and grandkids "waste" every day.

I said, "Wonderhubby, the TV is a screen."

He thought a minute and answered, "Oh."

— **Becky** —

HHATT Club members may whine about not having enough time alone—justified whining in most cases—but there can be an unexpected gift of freedom that comes with all this togetherness.

As it turns out, getting tired of each other may have an upside. Two of my sons work from home. Another son works three and a half days a week. Their wives are my heroes. Little do they know, but I've been studying and learning from them for years. I love watching how my sons and daughters-in-love get along while they're together, but I also enjoy seeing how they get along *not* together.

Couples who are separated for forty or more hours a week sometimes feel pressured to spend the majority of their together time together. Then comes the challenge of reaching compromises on how to spend your leisure time so everyone is happy. But when, as Kiley mentioned, your daily commute is from the bed to the desk chair in the corner of the bedroom, and when you sit across the table from each other (or—let's be realistic here—sit next to each other in front of the TV or with devices in hand) three meals a day, that pressure may disappear.

More accurately, that pressure may explode into an urgent need for time apart. And that's okay. Though let me add a note of caution right here: it's all too easy to take this to the extreme. Have you heard the latest trend in honeymoons? Some couples are choosing "solomoons" or "unimoons"—taking off on a post-wedding trip *without their new spouse.*

Another "creative" marriage form is LAT—living apart together. These are not couples separated by job demands or military service. These are people who prefer not sharing the same oxygen. Sociologists claim that LAT couples can be fully committed to each other even though they choose not to cohabit.

Umm . . . I don't think so.

Call me old-fashioned, but I just have to believe that if you want to keep the honeymoon feeling alive, you have to first experience one. Together. And I think there's a reason why God said in Genesis 2:24, "Therefore a man shall leave his father and his mother and hold fast to his wife, and they shall become one flesh" (ESV). How do you hold fast or enjoy one-fleshness if you live in Bugscuffle, Tennessee, and he's in Cheesequake, New Jersey? (Date night idea: Play "Can you top this?" with weird city names.)

Couples who work from home or are retired need to relax together, so we need the "What should we do for fun today?" discussions. But more time together can also mean less misplaced guilt when we want to head out and do our own thing.

> Couples who work from home or are retired need to relax together, so we need the "What should we do for fun today?" discussions. But more time together can also mean less misplaced guilt when we want to head out and do our own thing.

My daughter-in-law Adrianne says, "When Aaron starts talking about wanting to go metal detecting, I have to do my very best not to roll my eyes and groan about it. I love history, really enjoy antique stores, but I cannot wrap my brain around digging holes in the ground for an unknown. Of course, I also want him to do things he enjoys and finds relaxing, so I'll sometimes go along and read in the car while he 'relaxes,' or I'll set up a date with my sister so we're both getting to enjoy that time away from the kids."

Holly, married to my son Jeff, claims they "aren't super interesting" when it comes to relaxing. "Mostly our relaxation time each night looks like us sitting on the porch chatting, just the two of us or with friends. Some nights, though, he's watching a show while I'm reading a book. We both want each other to get good downtime alone, so we make it work. I love when he has time to golf because it's something he enjoys, and he supports my need for time with friends."

When it comes to planning vacations, Jeff and Holly both enjoy relaxing on the beach or by the pool, so planning is easy. But Holly also likes high-energy vacations spent exploring cities and jam-packing days with back-to-back adventure. My son is not a fan. So once a year Holly tries to plan a trip with girlfriends who enjoy the same kind of getaway. These two are also intentional in taking time for parent-child dates and weekend trips, something I wish we'd done more when our boys were young.

> We created "togetherness breaks" throughout the day . . . sometimes five minutes, sometimes a half hour. We walk around our little garden or watch the birds, hold hands, share something about our day. Sometimes we simply take time to laugh together. Because my husband and I started from a place of strength, this pattern of deliberate connection proved an easy step for us. But if you're starting point is a place of distance and disconnection, it will require hard work and intentionality to create these moments of intimacy throughout the day. It might feel awkward, frustrating, and even sad at first. But when you experience your first glimmer of connection, it will be completely worth your time and effort.
>
> —Tessa Afshar, award-winning author of *The Way Home: God's Invitation to New Beginnings*

My oldest son and his wife have worked from home together most of their married life. While homeschooling their three children, they enjoyed camping across the country, but Kristen's dream vacay has always been a trip to Disney. Even in his forties, at the mention of a week at a crowded theme park, Scott's face screws up exactly like it did when he was a toddler and tasted a lemon for the first time. (I've apologized profusely to my daughters-in-law for raising crowd-phobic introverts.) Over the years, when finances allowed, Kristen and the kids have enjoyed trips to Orlando while Scott stayed home, relishing the quiet.

A Guy's Perspective

- Keep a schedule. If your mind is focused on purposeful activities, you are less likely to follow your wife around expecting her to meet your needs.
- Create a routine with your wife that keeps you connected daily but doesn't take all day.
- Find a way to be physically active, even when you don't want to. Passively entertaining yourself all day will give your spouse the impression you're disengaged from the relationship, not just enjoying the moment.
- Find problems to solve that don't necessarily involve your wife.
- Look for something to do together you haven't done before that you both enjoy. Friends of ours decided to attend culinary school in France shortly after he retired because she loves to travel and he loves to cook.
- Be the person God wants you to be, not the person you are *tempted* to be in reaction to your spouse.
- Fight resentment. In most relationships, one spouse gives more than the other. If you aren't careful, you will build resentment and withhold affection. Over time, your mate will probably resent the fact that you have withheld what you used to freely share. Nobody wants mutual resentment to define their relationship! #crazycycle
- Spend time with your guy friends weekly. There is great power in the brotherhood!

—Bill Farrel, marriage relationship author and speaker

Dr. Snuggles is a runner. At the time I'm writing this, he's completed thirty-eight marathons and twenty half-marathons.

When people hear about those accomplishments, they are in awe. And then they turn to me. You know the question, right? My answer is, "Nope. Somebody's gotta cheer at the finish line."

I've tried running. Really, I have. I even bought a pair of running shoes for myself and wrapped them up and gave them to my hubby as a gift, along with the promise that I was finally going to "do this thing." I could see us, dressed in matching shorts, T-shirts, running belts, and zero-drop Altra Escalante 1.5 running shoes, panting down the road together, comparing PRs (personal records) and negative splits, and sharing energy gel packets and Gatorade. What a bonding experience. We'd travel the country in our RV, completing a marathon in every single state. It would be amazing! Except . . .

I *hate* running. I feel (and look) like a panting two-legged platypus waddling down the path. I watch people glide past our house, at one with the road, and try to copy their form. Nope. I have no form. My PR is a seventeen-minute mile.

I am *not* a runner. But . . . I do like to get on my bicycle. So sometimes when Dr. Snuggles heads out on a training run (sometimes, as in when I'm not home alone savoring the quiet), I'll hop on my bike and we'll enjoy nature together. I'll coast down the hills, whipping past him, ride a mile ahead, then turn around and meet him and we'll be side by side for a while, soaking up fresh air and sunshine.

Togetherness with freedom. A perfect balance.

> For us, the key has been to enjoy time together and time away. Having friends who want to go on an adventure with me equals a fun time for me (the extrovert) and alone time for him (the introvert).
>
> —Kendra Smiley, author and speaker

CHAPTER 6

But Honey, Both Our Names Are on the Mortgage

— Becky —

I remember the excitement of sitting down together to sign our first purchase agreement for a house. I remember lying awake talking to each other about where we'd hang that picture of Grandma Bessie and how we'd organize the kitchen cupboards. And my hubby shared his visions of furniture arrangements and knickknacks until long after midnight . . .

Okay, so that never really happened. Dr. Snuggles couldn't have cared less what cupboard the butter went in. As long as it *was* in the cupboard. (More on that later.) But I do remember the awake-until-after-midnight part . . . planning out every what-goes-where detail in high-def mental pictures to the backdrop of that soft snarfling sound in my right ear.

If your man is the kind without strong opinions about color schemes and wall hanging placement, you'll likely be fine if he is away from home during most daylight hours. The fact that you decide where the spatulas go or whether to hang filmy sheers or light-blocking blinds may rarely be an issue. But . . .

When you're both home, and he's squinting at sunlight streaming through lace valances and ricocheting off his computer screen . . . When he rearranges *your* cupboards for the sake of efficiency . . . When his creative inspiration creeps across the kitchen counter like a slow-moving glacier . . . tensions can arise.

It was relatively early in our marriage and Dr. Snuggles was working third shift (which is a whole lot like having a SITH. All. The. Time.) when I decided we needed a bookshelf in the living room. I can't remember for sure, but I'm going to claim, for purposes of justification, that I was pregnant and not working at the time. Because, you know, hormones. And finances . . . or the lack thereof.

I somehow got my hands on three orange crates in three different sizes. This was back before orange crates were cool, before you could buy a nice, matching, smoothly sanded set from Hobby Lobby for $71.96. These were the real deal—rough and splintery and probably housing tarantula eggs in the corners.

But they were free, and I was so proud of myself as I labored in our postage-stamp yard, hammering and painting. All black. It would go perfectly in our living room with burnt orange carpeting and curtains and black vinyl furniture. Sure, when I set it triumphantly in the fake-paneled room, it listed a bit to the left. And, yes, it was a tad bit wobbly, but with books on the bottom shelf to weigh it down . . .

I expected an "Attagirl!" or two when Dr. Snuggles crawled out of bed. I was not prepared for "What's that thing doing in our house?"

Those sad shelves became a source of gigantic contention in our not-yet-tested marriage. I never did fully grasp his problem with them. Hang on, I'll go ask him . . .

He says all he can remember is that it looked like we'd "piled up a bunch of crates in the living room."

Okay. With the perspective of time and without the intrusion of pregnancy hormones, I'll give him that. Still, he could have appreciated my motives. He says now he thought it was creative.

Pretty sure that word didn't surface at the time. Anyway, I stubbornly refused to move the shelves for at least a year. I think we ended up roasting hot dogs over my creativity.

Another thing in our first home. We needed an additional chair in that black and orange room. He wanted a blue one. Bright cobalt blue. I know I hurt his feelings when I stared at him with that you-have-got-to-be-kidding glare. For a guy who rarely cared about decor, why this? Why blue? This was the era of earth tones. Harvest gold, avocado, burnt orange. We didn't buy a blue chair. And I have since apologized, because, years later, when "they"—the people who decide such things for us—started combining blue and orange, I had to agree the combination was pretty groovy.

Then there's his picture-hanging thing. Every time we've moved, I have to do a quick sweep of the new house, scoping out nails on the walls the way a soldier searches a field for hidden mines. Because these little barbs of metal can set off big *booms* in our relationship. If I don't yank out nails left by the previous owners before he finds them, he'll hang a picture or a calendar on every single one. Doesn't matter where it is or if the picture ends up centered on the wall or up in a corner above the back door where someone once hung a spare key.

Once before a move, I made a deal with him. If he promised to not hang a single picture on an existing nail, I'd stop wearing flannel to bed for six months. It worked. At least, he held up his end of the bargain. I can't remember if I followed through for a full six months. I'm sure he remembers. Not going to go ask him.

I once read a book on home organizing that labeled people either "cleanies" or "messies." Since "opposites attract" isn't just a cliché, it's likely you're married to someone who is at a different end of the cleanie-messie spectrum. You may start making the bed before you get out of it, but he thinks there's nothing cozier than the sight of rumpled sheets and a concave pillow. Can we find middle ground?

In a famous quote from *Fiddler on the Roof*, Tevye says, "A bird may love a fish, but where would they build a home together?"[1] Are cleanies and messies destined to live in constant tension, one longing to soar high above the chaos while the other swims in it, never able to create a home that is suitable to both? Or is compromise a possibility?

My son Scott and daughter-in-law Kristen, the Disney loving/hating couple you met earlier, contend with this fish-bird tension daily. "Scott's an artist," Kristen says. "Although it makes no sense to me, he needs a little clutter and chaos to get his creative juices flowing. On the other hand, mess just shuts me down. Piles of stuff make me nervous and, honestly, a little depressed."

How do they handle it? Compromise. If he were in charge, my son's decor style would be "flannel and rust," but out of love for his wife he has created spaces for his artsy, rustic collections, and Kristen accepts that these not-shared spaces are "organized" in his way, not hers. "He has the workshop and his office, where I rarely set foot. His treasures and projects can pile up (or topple over) and it doesn't affect me in the slightest. Every so often, he sorts through his auction finds and cleans his spaces, but it's on his terms and never because I suggest it."

She admits that occasionally the stuff spreads into the house, spilling across the living room table. "That's fine for a little while," she says, "but he's aware that, per our agreement on shared space, the clock is ticking. The longer the pile stays, the more unhappy I get. He knows he can clean it up himself or one morning (usually day three) he will wake up and find his stuff has been neatly piled into a bushel basket and awaits him by the back door. Time for the mess to go home. It misses its friends in the workshop."

My daughter-in-law's words make me smile because I so clearly remember the day, a good two months after Scott left home and moved into his own apartment, that I had had enough of his junk still cluttering his old room. I packed it all up in big black trash bags, stuffed it in the van, and unceremoniously dumped it on his doorstep!

All the lessons we learned about sharing back in kindergarten come into play here. Like a five-year-old with a special toy Mom says we don't have to share, can we accept that the person sitting next to us in the circle also has something that's only his? Can we agree on "this little corner of the house is mine to keep the way I want, and that little corner is yours, but let's compromise on shared space"?

In chapter three, I suggested walking out your front door and coming back in with the mindset of your spouse. When it comes to home decor, how about stepping out together? Walk back in and take a tour of every shared space, talking about favorite colors, comfy groupings, pictures that make you both smile, mementos that remind you both of good times.

> A home was never intended to be a mash-up of two individuals' personal property.

What sparks *mutual* joy? What doesn't? A home was never intended to be a mash-up of two individuals' personal property.

Back in the day when monogrammed gifts were common for weddings, couples decorated bathrooms and bedrooms with towels and pillowcases embroidered with the first letter of their now shared last name flanked by two smaller letters—the initials of the bride's and groom's first names. Symbolic, isn't it? The two remain separate individuals, and yet they become one. Maybe you were gifted with matching coffee mugs labeled "His" and "Hers." As long as those labels don't cover every possession, they add to the ambience of our shared spaces.

If you're the winged creature who needs a she shed–tree house while he needs a man cave with a pond, creating your version of "my" spaces can make it much easier to compromise on the rooms we label "ours."

Philippians 2:4 says, "Let each of you look not only to his own interests, but also to the interests of others" (ESV). Not bad decorating advice.

> All the pungent pumpkin, flagrant floral, and superfluous citrus air fresheners in the world won't make your home as fresh as a daily spritzing of kindness.
>
> —Becky

— Cynthia —

Who would have thought an innocuous item like a cardboard box could start an argument?

He said, "Whatever you do, don't throw that box in the garage."

"I wouldn't throw it," I said. "But that's where cardboard boxes go to die."

"They don't belong in my garage."

"*Your* garage?"

"Whatever you don't want gets tossed in my garage, and I'm tired of it," he said.

"It's temporary, my beloved. It's like . . . the waiting room for the cardboard crematorium or recycling day."

"Not in my garage."

I probably should mention here that *our* four-space garage fits two cars, his workshop, and a one-stall mudroom.

"Where would you suggest I put things like that?" I asked sweetly. Relatively sweetly. "The bedroom? On top of the stove? In front of the TV?"

"I don't know. Just not in my garage, okay?"

I pondered and considered. Nothing clever came to me. Instead, I said, "Since this is all ours rather than his or hers, and since both our names are on the mortgage, what percentage of the garage do you think I should consider fair game for things like recyclables and my muddy boots and items I'm collecting to haul to the charity center? Could I have an eighth of a percent? That's all I'd need."

I completely understand not wanting someone else clogging up my space. But that word *my* had wormed its way too deep into the discussion. We compromised by deciding on a spot in the garage that wouldn't be in my husband's way but would be handy and visible enough that the items wouldn't be forgotten and become an accumulation.

"I live here too." We shouldn't have to say it, should we? Both the "a man's home is his castle" and "the garage belongs to the man, but the house belongs to the woman" mentalities veer wildly from God's heart for how a couple should perceive their home. *Their.* That's a clue.

Yes, we have taxidermied fish hanging on the walls of our family room. They were destined to live there anyway, so I purposed to choose a rustic Northwoods lodge theme for our decor. But my home office occupies a twelve-by-twelve-foot footprint that used to be a dining room. He has a work space. I have a work space. He has places in the house that cater to his need for leather couches the color of a horse saddle, and I have places with butter yellow walls and Blue Willow china. What's the real theme of the house? Compromise.

A friend once said that the goal of a home for a couple spending a lot of time there is to create an environment that is truly satisfying. Not simply comfortable but inspiring for all those who live within its walls. (Thanks, Janet Newberry.)

> **The goal of a home for a couple spending a lot of time there is to create an environment that is truly satisfying. Not simply comfortable but inspiring for all those who live within its walls.**

The key to having a happy home together is perspective. Maybe we no longer view ourselves as HHATT members (He's Home All the Time). Maybe we start viewing ourselves as WHATT members (We're Home All the Time). That family room with the giant TV and the giant fish? Multiple giant fish? It's a conversation starter. It's an inspiring place for my husband. Its saddle-colored couch is my favorite place to put my feet up. Its fireplace and coziness inspire both of us when we share it.

The spot where I find the most inspiration is the sunroom, which we created out of a screen porch. For the sake of making sure we both had places within the house that appealed to our individual aesthetics, we set money aside until we had enough to enclose the porch, install in-floor heating, and furnish the room with simple but non-fishing-camp-related items. It's graced with a small, apartment-sized sectional and a charming table for two, and is decorated in some of my favorite colors.

Creating a room like that wouldn't have been possible when our kids were young, or when the budget was even tighter than it is now. But because there's a spouse in the house almost all the time, and because I crave quiet, sunlight, and moments to myself, we made peace by remodeling a screen porch.

In Hebrews 13:21, we're told that the God of peace can "equip [us] with everything good for doing his will, and . . . work in us what is pleasing to him, through Jesus Christ."

Surely that promise extends to His influence on marriages that please Him too.

My husband says he doesn't "do" colors. He's not color-blind. He just doesn't care. Until he does. Remember "his" garage? When the mudroom part of it needed painting, I volunteered, since we've had a long-standing agreement that he paints the outside and I paint the inside. I'm a finesse painter. He's a climbs-on-tall-ladders kind of guy.

I'd fallen in love with a bright apple green paint I'd found on the clearance rack and surprised him with a freshly painted Granny Smith mudroom when he got home from work one day. He—the one who doesn't "do" colors—hated it. He couldn't explain why. It wasn't too feminine for his tastes. Maybe too bold? I didn't think so. But I knew he didn't like the color in a part of the garage he'd have to walk through multiple times a day.

So I did what every self-respecting woman would do. I fumed. Then, though he didn't insist or even ask me to, I repainted it in a light, unshocking yellow. Should I have had to? Not really. After all, both our names are on the mortgage.

But I repainted because I love him and care more about blessing him than I did about the hours it took or any inconvenience to me.

Love won.

And I used the leftover apple green to paint the tiny laundry room . . . since I knew he not only wouldn't see it every day but might not even know where it is.

Addendum to the story: He found the laundry room and has become an expert at throwing in a load or two when I'm on a business trip. Oh, and those cardboard boxes? As soon as they were disposed of, we had a sudden need for multiple boxes.

The hallways are tight? The bathroom's too small? There's nothing open about your home's concept? Where a HHATT member might say, "Stand aside. You're in my way," a WHATT Club member intent on finding mutually satisfying peace will say, "Excuse me, my love," or repaint a wall or two, and let love win.

> I will try to walk a blameless path, but how I need your help, especially in my own home, where I long to act as I should
> —Psalm 101:2 (TLB)

CHAPTER 7

At Least One of Us
Has to Be a Bomb Sniffer

— Cynthia —

Bomb-sniffing dogs aren't primarily sent into wreckage. Their purpose is to sniff out danger *before* it becomes heartbreak, before irreparable damage is done. In a WHATT (We're Home All the Time) marriage, either the husband or the wife (preferably both) needs to recognize danger early and take steps to ward it off.

Honestly, it's a requirement for a healthy marriage no matter how much or how little togetherness life hands us.

In the animal kingdom, judging from National Geographic and public television documentaries, physical intimacy comes naturally. Procreation and the act that leads to it do seem to originate in natural instincts for animals. I give you the gazelle, monitor lizards, and the dodo bird.

But that's a far cry from the intimacy that satisfies a human soul—a unique blend of physical, mental, emotional, and spiritual connection God intended a one-flesh relationship to nurture and maintain for a lifetime.

What kind of incendiary devices lie in ambush, on a mission to destroy marriages? It's a rhetorical question. We all know. Self-ishness. Score keeping. Even-Stevening the life out of being kind to one another. Resentment. Bitterness. Harsh words. Grudge bearing. Assuming the worst of your mate. Lack of communication. Unhealthy communication. Poor problem-solving skills. Lack of listening. Haughtiness. Impatience. Irritability. Taking ourselves too seriously. Control issues. Passive-aggressive speech and actions.

Relationship time bombs aren't always readily visible, but a good bomb sniffer doesn't require more than a whiff to detect potential trouble. It may work in the movies to cut a bomb's wires just as the countdown clock nears the final seconds before an explosion. Doesn't work so well to wait that long with a marriage detonation device. We have to stay alert and sniff them out before defusing becomes necessary. If you've watched reruns of *The Andy Griffith Show*, you may recall Deputy Fife's iconic, "Nip it. Nip it, nip it, nip it in the bud!" Who knew Fife's encouragement to deal with issues early would apply so well to disarming potential destruction before it has a chance to mess with a two-spouses-in-the-house scenario?

One of the best bomb-defuser tools is humor. But only when it's shared. It has a detonation effect if it's implemented *against* our spouse.

Have you ever tried to self-assemble a gluten-free Reuben sandwich . . . on your lap . . . in the car? Is it just me? After months of stuck-in-the-house-together togetherness, we ventured out for a quick trip to town and a couple of errands. The conclusion of the errands happened to coincide with an approaching mealtime. I love when that happens.

"Want to grab lunch at Culver's before we head home?" Wonderhubby asked.

"You should know by now I never turn down an invitation not to cook." (And this spoken by a woman who began cooking for her siblings and parents when she was twelve. Oh, wait. That's why I'm so tired of it!)

We idled our car in the extra-long line for the drive-through. We'd resigned ourselves to eating in the parking lot, which overlooked the bowling alley. Considerably less romantic than if we'd had a lake view or perhaps a mountain vista.

Even with a paper take-out bag as a table, it was surprisingly awkward to open the single-serve, cellophane-sealed gluten-free bun, then pile it with corned beef, smear on Thousand Island dressing, add just enough of the little packet of sauerkraut to flavor the concoction without stinking up the car, and then slide on the not very melty Swiss cheese.

I hadn't taken more than one bite before something dribbled out—part of it landing on my shirt and the other on the paper bag "table."

Wonderhubby said, "I can't take you anywhere nice."

Admittedly, some days I might not find a comment like that humorous. But he meant it as a joke, and I took it as one. And we'd committed to looking for the humor in otherwise humorless situations. We laughed harder than we had in a long time. It was obviously not a condemnation of my neatness skills but commentary on how ridiculous the scene must have looked from a bird's-eye—or God's—view. Forced to eat in the car, in the parking lot, and charged with creating my own sandwich in my lap. I think even the bowling alley was laughing with us.

We laughed *together*. It defused what could have been a frustrating moment.

For years, one of my heart's desires for our marriage was to share consistent times of prayer with my husband. We prayed together over meals and when someone we loved was in crisis.

But I hungered for the kind of spiritual intimacy that develops when a couple creates a daily habit of praying together. I asked. We'd succeed at sustaining a nightly prayer time for two or three days in a row, but then we'd fall back into old habits. I could have stepped into the role of prayer-reminder person, but that felt like pushing my husband into it rather than a mutual decision. So I made *prayer* a matter of prayer.

I stopped mentioning my longing for us to pray together every day and simply reminded God of my heart's desire.

Twenty-four years later—that's right—my husband suggested we spend some time every evening praying together. And we've sustained the sacred, beautiful, intimate, relationship-sealing practice. After the "amen," he kisses me on the lips, on my nose, and on my forehead. The forehead kiss feels like a sweet symbol of blessing. Worth the wait. Worth waiting for God to do the pushing.

Proactive bomb sniffing can prevent relationship fallout that throws shrapnel, creates wounds and scars, and leaves marriage partners choking on its dust.

My bomb sniffing noted that our relationship could be stronger if we were consistent in prayer together. But it also noted that if I forced it, a secondary explosive device might have detonated—disrespect. It's as important to proceed cautiously as it is to recognize a spot of vulnerability or an unmet expectation.

Proactive bomb sniffing can prevent relationship fallout that throws shrapnel, creates wounds and scars, and leaves marriage partners choking on its dust. One of the best ways to sniff out problems is to ask these questions:

- Are you following through on good intentions to maintain a consistent schedule of date nights?
- Do you *hope* to find time together or *plan* time together?
- Are you connecting on matters of faith beyond sitting side by side in weekly worship services?
- Do you check in with each other with non-interruptive "day brighteners" or evidence of your love?

- Do you share the same definition of *non-interruptive*?
- Do you share the same definition of what kind of thing brightens your spouse's day?
- Are you continually working at growing in your methods of communicating with one another, focusing on listening rather than on being heard?
- Do you know each other's "why"?

I purposefully left that last question at the end to help emphasize it. It undergirds all the others. *Why* is it important for him to make the coffee or for her to take a nap midafternoon, or for him to watch CNN or for her *not* to watch CNN?

Why does she retreat to another room when he starts telling a friend, stranger, or hardware store clerk the stories about his adventures in Canada, the ones she knows by heart?

Why is saving a nickel on gas so important to him?

If we recognize the smell of danger for a relationship in its beginning years, then in its retirement years (note: relationships don't retire), or when working from or caregiving at home, we're better able to steer around that throat-clenching, heart-thumping ticking sound before *three, two, one, boom!*

Not all that long ago, I took advantage of a warm day and a little free time to work on cleaning up the garden. I tugged and pulled and snipped at stray blackberry brambles and weeds, raking garden debris into a big, dusty pile.

Before long, I sensed strange droplets of moisture pooling on my forehead and around my neck. The rare perspiration! My husband was sitting on the deck. Watching me work. Watching me strain. Watching me struggle. I did not know his why nor did I care to, at the moment.

When I was finished in the garden, he headed for the shed to try once more to get the lawn tractor started after several days of unsuccessful attempts and makeshift fixes. In the house, I cleaned up—but not inside. Inside my heart, I was more than a little miffed that my beloved took pleasure in watching me work rather than stepping in to help.

God raked something out of my soul. What would be the opposite of what I felt like doing right then? I could take him a glass of cold water and ask, "Is there any way I can help you?" Complete reverse of my natural inclination. So I figured it had to be God.

Obeying God and blessing my husband changed the atmosphere, at least the atmosphere hovering around me. Snipped that wire and defused a bomb.

Nipped it. Nipped it, nipped it, nipped it.

Think I'll try that again someday soon.

Things my husband, Phil, does when I'm in my office working:

- Brings me a wiggly frog he found while mowing
- Asks if I can come out to play
- Decides to remodel something on podcast-recording day
- Talks through the French door instead of opening it to ask a question
- Bangs more doors than an army of teenage boys
- Totally redeems himself by asking if he can cook supper

—Michelle Rayburn, author of *Classic Marriage: Staying in Love as Your Odometer Climbs*

— Becky —

"Why do I always have to be the one to buy the marriage book, start the define-the-relationship talk, or suggest counseling or a marriage retreat? Why can't he be the one to show some initiative when things aren't going well?"

Over the years, as I've chatted with friends or counseled women in less-than-perfect marriages (as if "perfect" and "marriage" were not oxymorons), I've heard many variations on this same question. And, yes, I've posed it myself.

> Just the fact that we rub shoulders more often due to retirement increases the odds of friction.
>
> —Tony B.

Cynthia talked about knowing our spouse's whys. "Why do I always have to be the one . . . ?" is a good why to start with. I don't have all the answers (because "perfect" and "me" are absolutely not synonyms), but I do have some suggestions.

1. *He might be just fine.* This one I know from personal experience. There have been seasons when I felt neglected and wondered if my husband had grown tired of me. Passion had flatlined. Was romance going to be a distant memory from now on? Did he even still love me?

And, no, you're not alone if you've ever marked on the calendar the last time you made love or he said those three precious words. (Ouch . . . did I actually just admit that in print?) After days, or weeks, of thinking we've come to the purely platonic point in our marriage, I'll finally get serious about praying (as opposed to simply whining to God) and then I'll find the courage to have a DTR conversation.

I've learned over the years that the way to start a meaningful define-the-relationship talk is not "We need to talk!" Most men would rather go toe-to-toe with a category-five hurricane than be trapped in the house with that statement hanging in the air. If you pick the right moment (when he's fed and rested and not in the middle of watching a hockey game) and quietly ask, "Are we okay?" you probably won't get a wall of defensiveness in response.

But you may get a blank stare. Because he has no idea what you're talking about.

I've seen it more than once. I'd been wondering if he's on the verge of leaving me and he'd been thinking we're just fine.

Usually, once I tell him how I've been feeling and he has a chance to explain, I discover there's a reasonable explanation for the distance I perceived. Maybe he's been distracted by a project or worried about finances. Sometimes the only explanation is that I'm a romance writer and I have a picture in my mind of how romance is supposed to look after half a century—a picture that doesn't quite match his. We talk it out. We hug, we kiss. He says those three little words. And we're back on track.

My advice? Talk. Long before you start checking the closet to see if he's packed his suitcase.

2. *Women are more intuitive.* I know, this sounds horribly sexist. But there's science behind it. In a study led by the University of Cambridge, with collaborators from Australia, France, the Netherlands, and the United States, researchers tested ninety thousand people to find out if there were gender variants associated with cognitive empathy—that is, our ability to understand another person's emotional state just at a glance. Subjects were shown different photographs of people's eyes, then were asked to label that person's mood. The results: women consistently outperformed men.[1]

Science doesn't have an explanation for this yet, but I think God does. He created males to have more muscle mass and protective instincts that are different from ours. He gave both men and women oxytocin, also known as the love hormone, which is associated with empathy, trust, and relationship building. But in general, women have it in higher doses.

My advice? Buy the relationship book. Suggest the getaway or a few sessions of counseling. Instead of getting frustrated when he can't sense the C-4 in your marriage, thank God that you were created with heightened senses.

3. *You might just be bored.* Sometimes when we're feeling something's "off" in our marriage, it's really just a case of the blahs.

As I was writing this book, my friend Leah's husband was unexpectedly required to work from home. In the midst of this abundance of togetherness, I asked her how she handled it when she sometimes felt her marriage was far from thriving.

"We try to plan a date night to reconnect and get away from the stressors at home," Leah said. "It can be hard for me to relax when I see laundry, dishes, and accumulating mess. Because we're blessed with a teenage daughter who can watch the younger ones, we have the freedom to get away together —even if it's curbside pickup at our favorite restaurant and eating in the car."

Leah told me her parents always talked about love and marriage as a sine wave or roller coaster. There are low points—seasons that require survival mode—but if you hold on, the highs will come again. "Josh and I can grind through some hard seasons knowing that the fun, enjoyment, and love we have for each other and with each other will rise to the surface again."

> My wife and I decided to go on two-mile walks several times a week. We both live a very busy lifestyle. We walk on a rails-to-trails path not far from our home, enjoying the path and the beauty nature provides for us along the way.
>
> As we start our walks, we share each other's events and concerns that we experienced that day. As we turn and head for home, we make a conscious choice to encourage each other and discuss plans for the future. These walks provide us with exercise and ensure we have quality time we both need. We have the freedom to express our daily hardships and catch up, but then as we turn toward home, we express our appreciation for each other and how God has blessed us.
>
> —Dr. Mike

My advice? Sometimes relationship stagnation is the problem, and time alone together is all that's required. In a perfect world, you'd take turns coming up with ideas or plan all your date nights together. It's hard when you feel like adding some sizzle is always up to you. I think we're in agreement that trying to change our men is God's job and not ours, so if the alternative to taking the initiative is staying in boredom, isn't it worth letting go of "Why do I always have to be the one to _____?" and moving on to planning something fun?

Get dressed up and pretend for an evening that you're not together all the time. Look up marriage conversation-starter questions online. Flirt like you don't pick up his dirty socks every morning and he doesn't see you sleeping with your mouth hanging open.

> **Get dressed up and pretend for an evening that you're not together all the time.... Flirt like you don't pick up his dirty socks every morning and he doesn't see you sleeping with your mouth hanging open.**

4. *He might be hiding something.* What do you do when your heightened senses pick up something ticking, and it's getting louder by the second? Any reason for forced togetherness can expose a spouse who's sneaking off to "work out" or texting in the middle of the night. Affairs, and other forms of betrayal, come to light. Pornography, gambling addictions, alcoholism, eating disorders, online shopaholism, and illicit drug use are harder to hide when you're sharing close quarters.

And let's be honest here. That list of secret sins applies to women too. A 2018 study found that 73 percent of women reported internet porn use in the last six months.[2] A 2013 survey discovered that 57 percent of online gamblers in the United States are female.[3] Add to this the ease of online shopping creating the potential for addiction, or the "convenience" of finding a male "friend" on the internet, and we have to admit we are just as vulnerable as our men.

My advice? Before the bomb counter gets down to zero, get help. Talk to a pastor or trusted counselor. Don't offer to be your husband's accountability partner. He needs another man, someone who isn't afraid to be tough. With support of your own, you can work toward forgiveness and, if he's willing, become his biggest cheerleader.

I know this may sound trite to someone in the midst of a true marriage crisis, but God is the author of second chances. And grace. And mercy. And forgiveness. And reconciliation. He wrote the Book on it.

And if *you're* the one whose sin comes to light? Pray. Seek help and accountability. Be transparent with your spouse. Keep praying.

In Song of Songs 2:15, the Shulammite bride-to-be says, "Catch for us the foxes, the little foxes that ruin the vineyards, our vineyards that are in bloom." She's just been extolling her fiancé's wonderful features. What is she talking about here?

Foxes are creatures that can destroy vineyards. The "vineyards that are in bloom" symbolize their growing love. In other words, she's saying, "Catch those things that could wreck our relationship. Let's put protective measures in place to stop anything from damaging our love for each other."

Whether your foxes are small things like taking each other for granted or big, terrifying creatures like addiction or infidelity, our prayer is that, with God's help, you can catch them before they do irreparable harm. God is the hero of your story, and its author. Let Him write a great "ever after" and a breathtaking "from this day forward" for you.

CHAPTER 8

The Sins Febreze Can't Quite Cover

— Becky —

When I'm the last one to get up in the morning, I make the bed. When *he's* the last one to get up in the morning, I make the bed.

I leave cupboard doors open while I'm cooking. I leave water running long after the pan is filled. I fold clothes on our bed . . . and they're still there when it's time to crawl in.

He takes on a project (like peeling the bubbling plaster hidden by the curtain under the kitchen windowsill) while I'm cooking and cleaning for company.

He sits in the recliner when he comes back from a long run. In sweaty clothes. And those clothes, when we're sharing 260 square camper feet, are damp, they're smelly, and they're draped over everything to dry out.

In our otherwise fairly neat bedroom, the built-in vanity I never use for vain purposes is a catchall. Scarves, jewelry, lotion bottles, hair product, receipts, and other stuff emptied from pockets. A veritable natural pharmacy sprouts next to his sink. Vitamin bottles that should be on a shelf surround the basin like sentinels guarding the teeny tiny hairs littering the porcelain. And those hairs . . .

Care to add your list of annoying habits to mine?

Remember when we asked you to find out the why behind his behavior? It's time to turn the why question on yourself. Why does the sound of his chewing bug you? Why do you feel like screaming as you wipe his sticky fingerprints off the grape jelly jar . . . again?

And then there's the flip side: Why do I keep forgetting to shut cupboard doors? Why don't I fold clothes in the laundry room? Why do you keep sticking the butter in the fridge when you know that "stone-hard butter" is one of his most explosive triggers? (Oh, wait, that's not you. That was me. But I stopped that annoying habit two days after our honeymoon.)

Unlike with oysters, irritation in a marriage is incapable of producing a pearl.

> **Unlike with oysters, irritation in a marriage is incapable of producing a pearl.**

Why do some of our SITH's quirks irritate us? And especially so when we're occupying the same space for an extended period of time? Let's look at possible reasons.

It's legit: The Declaration of Independence does not declare that anyone has the right to life, liberty, and the pursuit of a frog prince figurine collection that fills every nook and cranny of the house. It does not grant the right to sing show tunes in the car while your spouse is reading, or to start adopting stray cats when your spouse is allergic.

Some things do need to change. A calm discussion, using "I feel" statements rather than "You make me feel" accusations, is a good place to start. If that doesn't work, you might need a neutral third party to intervene.

It's something else: Ever wonder why his soft humming while you're playing cards is sometimes comforting and other times grates on you like squeaking Styrofoam? There's likely another issue simmering in your brain. He made that rude comment about your mom. It was his turn to put the trash out, but he left it for you. He hasn't said "I love you" in . . . let me check the calendar . . . five days. It's also possible that everything he's doing irritates you because he's not doing what you want him to do. That's the situation Leah found herself in.

Leah had projects she wanted to get done around the house. Though her pastor husband, Josh, had a busy at-home work schedule with online meetings and earning his MBA, he agreed to help her paint the trim on the house.

From the beginning, she could tell he wasn't passionate about the project. "That whole first day he kept talking about removing our normal (slightly out of tune but otherwise perfectly fine) piano and converting it into a stand in which to put the electric piano, and that the old piano could then also double as a desk," Leah says. "I wasn't on board, but I told him that would be a fine project for the *future*. Next thing I know, he's ripped apart the piano and parts are strewn all over the living room."

Over the next few days, Josh helped (a bit) with the projects on Leah's list, but the piano overhaul consumed most of his free time and cut into family time.

Before long Leah found herself thinking thoughts she knew were lies: "Josh doesn't care about the things I care about. We can *never* get along."

Can you relate? I can.

Leah finally talked to a trusted friend who patiently listened and then prayed with her. Less than twelve hours later, she was once again viewing Josh as her friend, partner, and love. Yes, the trim did finally get painted, and she says, "I finally admitted that a piano converted into a desk would be handy."

So, before you blast him for that little thing that's annoying you this second, do an "irritation inventory." What else is going on? If all is well between the two of you, stooping to pick up dirty socks or listening to him singing "Send in the Clowns" in the shower won't increase your blood pressure a single point.

Though it goes without saying that your spouse, like mine, has far more annoying quirks than we righteous women do, it's only fair that we admit we're doing a couple of things that bug them too. So it's time to turn the tables and ask, Why do I keep doing the things I know irritate him?

Let's look at a couple of possible reasons.

I'm clueless: I seriously don't realize three cupboard doors are open . . . until he walks in and quietly starts shutting them. Or bumps his head on one. What can we do about these ingrained habits? Well, I could use my son Scott's defense—"Mess feeds the creative muse." (Where oh where did he get that?) Or I could leave myself a note: *"Close cupboards."* Note writing or tying strings around fingers works for just about anything. But be patient with yourself. "They" say it takes twenty-one days to break a habit.

I'm doing it on purpose: Now we're getting to some nitty-gritty ugly. But we've all been there, haven't we? "I'll show him. If he's going to keep doing *that*, I'm going to start doing *this*!"

I've only found one thing that breaks that cycle: repentance. We need to get on our knees before the God who loves us and loves the concept of marriage and fess up. And then make an about-face. Need help? How about this reminder? "But the fruit of the Spirit is love, joy, peace, forbearance, kindness, goodness, faithfulness, gentleness and self-control" (Galatians 5:22–23).

Ever read that verse and say "Ouch"? I have. It would be easy to use it as a checklist for our spouses, wouldn't it? Love? Not so much today. Gentleness? Needs some work. Self-control? That remote has been in his hand for five hours straight! But God didn't allow these words to be written to give us a guideline for measuring our spouse's quirks and failings. This is a list of gifts given to you and to me and to our mates. Gifts that we can choose to use or ignore. How about we make a pact to ask God every day to help us be more loving, joyful, peaceful, patient, kind, good, faithful, gentle, and self-controlled in our marriages?

— Cynthia —

How is a spouse like a bad college roommate? He eats what you planned for lunch or supper. Neglects to replace the roll of toilet paper. Leaves messes that become an embarrassment to you . . . or a health hazard. Doesn't leave a note about where he's going. Considers it an imposition to take your package to the post office when he's driving past it on his way to . . . well, *not work*. Uses the last of the coffee beans without scribbling "coffee" on the grocery list a foot away.

None of us wants to be known as the spouse who's more like a bad college roommate than a caring life mate. But it's all too easy to slip into habits devoid of common courtesy, especially when we're tired or stressed or overloaded, or tired and stressed and overloaded *and* have a 24/7 live-in spouse.

> **None of us wants to be known as the spouse who's more like a bad college roommate than a caring life mate.**

Yes, it's a very good thing to have a spouse, to have the love of your life under the same roof. Other people have written books about how wonderful it is in retirement to finally have time for "just the two of you." Read those books next. But Becky and I want to serve as voices for those who are *aware* of the wonderful side but are low on oxygen at the moment. Or are building their reserves for the next time the kitchen seems to have shrunk overnight. Or the living room.

I was a newlywed when I experienced a Leah-like story. While her husband tore apart a piano in her living room, my husband laid an old blanket on the carpet in the living room of our honeymoon apartment and dismantled a motorcycle. Yeah. The man I had to remind myself I loved. Our small apartment—about the size of a motorcycle—seemed dreamy before that. I hadn't even considered decorating with motorcycle parts, most of which smelled like motor oil, dirt, gasoline, or a combo of all three. Did I mention our four-by-six-foot kitchenette was open to the living room?

> When a couple says, "It's stuffy in here," God doesn't say, "Then leave." He says, "Open a window."
>
> —Cynthia

Today—as in, *today*—I realized that forgiving him for that wasn't all that noble of me. The man didn't have a garage. We had one car, which I needed to commute to work in another town. The rusty motorcycle was his only means of transportation to school and his part-time job. We didn't even have a carport or a driveway, only a numbered spot in a large communal parking lot. He had no space to take it apart. And he had, after all, thoughtfully laid a blanket on the carpet.

Reflecting back across all those years, with a thousand offenses and apologies between, I thought I'd been wronged. But he was just a newly married man trying to hold things together and repair what we couldn't afford to have looked at by a mechanic.

What would I tell that new bride now, if I could? I'd tell her to pre-forgive everything that man would ever do in the future . . . which is where I'm living now.

And to pre-forgive myself for how many times I would need God's grace to cover my failures.

Forgive me, Wonderhubby, for I have sinned against you so many times when I didn't know enough, didn't understand your why, didn't tell myself to get out of the way so I could see your heart better.

There. That ought to do it. I'm cured. I'll never again be neglectful, impatient, irritable, or selfish-disguised-as-self-preserving.

The phone rings. Excuse me a minute. Yes, I'm writing and he's doing nothing at the moment. And the phone is a room away from me and eight feet away from him. But he always expects me to be the one to answer the phone when it rings.

So apparently . . . I'm not cured. But a long time ago I pre-forgave. I just needed the reminder.

What will it take to navigate the square footage of our home (and the cubic footage of a marriage) when all-the-time togetherness feels like a too-tight T-shirt woven of steel wool, superglue, and rose thorns? A whole lot of pre-forgiveness, learning and relearning, reminding ourselves of what we know is right and uplifting and relationship-strengthening.

What will it take? It's more of a Who than a what. God not only instructs but empowers us to consider the needs of others, to reinstall lost mouth filters (see James 4), to forgive abundantly (even pre-forgive), to honor each other—and in doing so, to honor Christ.

A simple formula? "Give it to Jesus. Ta-da! Marital bliss."

Yeah, no.

God's Thoughts About the Gift of Consideration

Let your speech always be gracious, seasoned with salt, so that you may know how you ought to answer each person. (Colossians 4:6 ESV)

Out of the same mouth come praise and cursing. My brothers and sisters, this should not be. (James 3:10)

Kind words are like honey—sweet to the soul and healthy for the body. (Proverbs 16:24 NLT)

Make allowance for each other's faults, and forgive anyone who offends you. Remember, the Lord forgave you, so you must forgive others. (Colossians 3:13 NLT)

Outdo one another in showing honor. (Romans 12:10 ESV)

Even the most nurturing soul is wired for self-protection. We don't need to be taught to blink when something comes flying toward our eyes. We don't take classes to learn how to jump back when we touch something too hot or to shield our eyes from too-bright sunlight. We are built by our Creator with instincts to keep us safe.

But sometimes, self-preservation morphs into selfishness or self-absorption. We're well aware of our own needs. Not so much the needs of the person breathing more than 50 percent of the allotted air in our home.

But at least some of our faux pas are less sinister than that. We may not have enough information to realize that the straw we're stepping on is our spouse's last one. Or that the minor infraction of neglecting to pick up eggs while at the store means that the special dessert he was planning to make (let's say *he*, because I *swan*—as they say in the South—ain't nothin' better lookin' than a man doin' the cookin'. I wouldn't know, but I've heard) is ruined forever and always, world without end, amen.

> To the non-cook: If the kitchen is foreign territory, don't be afraid to ask where the cheese grater goes. YouTube can teach you everything from how to boil an egg to ways to throw a dinner party for twenty.
>
> —Becky

Pre-forgiveness. Consideration. Overt kindness. A formulaic answer for marital bliss? No.

Thriving as a couple will take faithfulness in all arenas—mentally, emotionally, spiritually, and physically. Surviving the little annoyances and the larger isn't-that-considered-torture-according-to-the-Geneva-convention? ones—like passing gas under the covers—will always be an exercise in "lov[ing] each other with genuine affection, and tak[ing] delight in honoring each other" (Romans 12:10 NLT).

Take delight in honoring each other. That passage from the

Bible was specifically talking about relationships between people who become "family" by way of faith in Jesus Christ. How much more should that concept apply to those who become family when they pledge their lives to one another in marriage?

Prefer one another. Honor one another. Consider one another. Maybe it is a formula after all.

Mercy's Laws (as Opposed to Murphy's Laws) of Marriage

- It's not only appropriate but wise to pre-forgive your spouse. In his classic *Mere Christianity*, C. S. Lewis wrote, "Every one says forgiveness is a lovely idea, until they have something to forgive."[1]
- If you get disgusted with your mate, it's likely you'll do something before the day's over that will frustrate him. Don't let disappointment grow moldy and turn into disgust.
- Remember that whatever flaws you see in your spouse are really strengths in disguise, or strengths in a temporary bad mood.
- Everything God wants to see happen in a church, in the world, He wants to see happen in families and couples—unity, forgiveness, kindness, compassion, humility, respect . . .
- It's hard to stay angry at someone you're praying for.

—Cynthia[2]

CHAPTER 9

We're Dancing, but He's Listening to Different Music

— Cynthia —

Did you know that the distance between competitive ice dancing partners should not exceed two arm lengths at any time during a routine? At the beginning and end of the free dance, the couple may separate for up to ten seconds without restriction on the distance. At any other time, each separation of no more than two arm lengths must not last longer than five seconds.[1]

Daily life isn't like that, nor should it be. I can see the comedy routine now—a husband and wife handcuffed together so they don't violate the "no distance between us" rule. Toothbrushing is a disaster unless one of them is left-handed. No, wait. Still a disaster if the dominant hands are handcuffed. Can you imagine any aspect of the day that wouldn't be more complicated if you were physically (or virtually, as in the case of ice dance competitors) handcuffed to your partner?

That dogmatic togetherness is not the kind of sweet marital dance God intended us to enjoy. In biblical times, husbands and wives spent much of their day apart, engaged in activities that kept their households provided for, their children fed and educated.

The beauty of ice dancing is synchronization of movement, but not always duplication. Brief moments apart, then coming back together. Practiced movements that allow each partner to progress through the program in a harmonious, graceful way.

Fans of ice dancing often refer to the Torvill and Dean 1984 Olympic gold medalists' performance to *Boléro* as the quintessential example of the sport at its best. Intimate. Powerful. Elegant. The two moved as one, but also as individuals responding to the other. If you haven't seen that classic performance online, it might be worth your time to watch it through the lens of what it can teach us about moving in sync with one another when we're home all the time.[2]

Ballroom dance instructors make it a point to encourage those whose first lessons seem awkward, when inexperienced students are literally stepping on each other's toes. Not so unlike a married couple vying for the shower, or the last piece of leftover chicken, or the spot behind the wheel. Instructors lavish encouragement because they know it takes practice to move in sync with instead of stumbling over one another.

The dance analogy may be an easier one to identify with if we imagine one partner attempting a waltz and the other line dancing. Both are listening to music. Both are moving their feet. But someone could get hurt.

It's a skilled dance pair who can step into the narrow spaces between the other's feet. It takes practice, not just longevity. It's more than number of years spent together.

We can, though, learn to listen for the music playing in our partner's head.

A dance instructor might show uncommon patience as his students slowly progress from counting out loud and staring at their feet to feeling the music and gliding across the floor together. The instructor might tell the husband, "You don't have to call out your directions to your wife. The light pressure of your hand on the small of her back is enough for her to anticipate where the two of you are heading next."

Just as a professional dancer communicates unspoken elegance, it is possible for us to synchronize our marriage moves so our relationship becomes a form of worship that honors God, enriches us, and serves as an example to others who are still in the tripping-over-each-other stage.

> **It is possible for us to synchronize our marriage moves so our relationship becomes a form of worship that honors God, enriches us, and serves as an example to others who are still in the tripping-over-each-other stage.**

Wonderhubby and I have been working on repairing the hundred-year-old hardwood floors that were exposed during our elbow-room-means-more-than-eighteen-inches renovation. He has other things he'd rather be doing. So do I. But the project is teaching us better emotional and relational dance routines.

Some of it is synchronizing our skill sets (he's better with a circular saw and I'm better at fitting the puzzle pieces of new boards to replace missing or fire-damaged floorboards). We take turns encouraging one another during the long, slow, handcrafted process. Yes, handcrafted. We're making the replacement boards from wood my husband salvaged from the large maple tree that once graced our yard. When he removes a damaged floorboard, I'm at the ready with the vacuum cleaner wand to rid the area of sawdust, like a nurse responding to a surgeon's request for "Suction!"

I measure wrong. He forgives me.

He scuffs a board when the circular saw bucks. I forgive him.

Long, hard days. Complicated-calculation dance steps as we try to make the most of our limited supply of maple and figure out how to inject Botox into a floor showing its age.

But we're listening to the same music. It's a project we care about and one we know will be worth it in the end. The ability to use lumber from a tree we knew adds a layer of sentimentality.

But what if neither of you recognize the song, and the rhythm is completely erratic and hard to follow? What if the season you're in is one you not only didn't expect but certainly didn't want? What if you're together so much because one is caregiving for the other due to illness or injury or surgery? Or because it's dangerous beyond the doors of your home? Or because of a job loss? Or dueling job losses have you planted at home whether you like it or not?

You hold each other and sway back and forth. It's still dancing.

Fluid, ballet-like dancers move across the floor, never too far from each other but never tripping over each other either, with both opposing actions and mirrored actions, listening to the music and to each another. When the choreography requires it, they create space, not distance.

Marriage is like that. We learn to respect the other's personal space without letting it become distance.

— **Becky** —

There are two sides of me
Each needing equal time:

Give me music	*Give me space*
Give me color	*Give me quiet*
Give me rhyme	*Give me time*

Yep, another poem dredged from the archives. I think I wrote this in my freezing-in-winter, cooking-in-summer unfinished attic "office" while Dr. Snuggles and our boys were downstairs watching *Dukes of Hazard*. Back when I felt like the crazy busy of being a wife and mom was suffocating my free-spirited, hippie wannabe, flowers-in-her-hair, barefoot poet persona.

I wanted to write. I wanted time, and enough quiet to hear my own thoughts. Or the freedom to play my vinyl *Parsley, Sage, Rosemary and Thyme* record at full volume.

I wanted my husband to understand all this. I wanted him to instinctively know when I needed alone time. I wanted him to make it happen.

My husband is not a poet. He didn't come into our marriage preprogrammed with the need to build a nest of pillows and cozy blankets, furnished with books and journals and an IV drip of Red Zinger tea sweetened with raw honey.

He doesn't need alone time . . . so he doesn't recognize the need in me.

Correction: he *didn't* recognize it.

He also didn't (intensely past tense!) recognize my need for time with girlfriends or other writers. Once, about ten years into our marriage, when he was a full-time chiropractic student and I was a stay-at-home mom, I bent to kiss him good-bye as I headed out for a monthly writers' meeting. His smile was tight as he said, "I just wish you could do these things on your own time."

On my own . . . *WHAT?* (I would have used 164-point font here if space allowed.)

We had three children at the time. I repeat: my own *what?*

A friend of mine calls the kind of interactions that ensued "intense fellowship." Such a nice euphemism for "Are. You. Kidding. Me? When in the world do I get time—for a breath, or a bathroom break, or a shower—to call my own? Why don't *you* . . ."

How I wish I could rewind and erase that scene. What if I had stopped to read between his lines? What if, instead, I'd heard what he didn't express? "I've been in class all day. I'm exhausted and I've got homework. Tucking the kids in is going to cut into study time, which means I'll get to bed late and I've got that exam tomorrow . . ." Or maybe, "We don't have enough time together as it is. I miss you. I get that you need this, but are there any writers' meetings during the day? We can afford a sitter for a couple of hours."

Or what if he'd actually said those words . . . long before I was walking out the door in a huff?

We've learned over the years. We've studied each other's rhythms and found ways to move in sync at times and to separate at other times. While he dances to the beat of a political talk show in the living room, I'll unload the dishwasher while grooving to praise music or a podcast on the craft of writing. We have a good balance of time with our friends, pursuing our own interests, and time together.

But sometimes, just when you think you've got the beat memorized and you've rehearsed all those steps, your spouse swipes to a different playlist. The guy who used to sit in the car with the kids waiting for you to stop gabbing with every single person in the church foyer is now the one inside chatting with the pastor while you're sitting in the car with a growling stomach and steam pouring out of your ears . . . in an empty parking lot.

That's not hypothetical. I used to be way more extroverted than I am now. I had a serious case of FOMO. Fear of missing out kept me on the go. Add in fear of saying no (FOSN doesn't really have a ring to it, does it?), and if there was an event at church, I was there. Often at the cost of being with family and getting needed rest. Fast-forward a couple of decades, and he's the one saying, "Hey, we should go . . ." or "We should invite . . ." while I'm the one with the tight smile.

Learning to embrace the differences adds color and rhyme to what might otherwise be a rather drab relationship.

I love being with people . . . once I'm with them. It's the planning ahead while I'm home in my nest hugging a cup of Red Zinger that's so much harder than it once was.

Accepting that our life rhythms will change, much like the sine waves Leah mentioned in chapter seven, will keep us from being blindsided. Learning to embrace the differences adds color and rhyme to what might otherwise be a rather drab relationship. My mother was known for saying, "If the two of you always agree on everything, one of you is unnecessary." Good words. Not sure she knew she was quoting William Wrigley Jr.[3]

> Ultimately, we had to figure out a system that worked for both of us. We had to refine old patterns to adjust to our new situation. Because I work from home, it is easier for my husband to create boundaries around my time. As a veteran professional, he understands the importance of deadlines. A lot of our harmony is owed to his sensitivity to my needs as I work.
>
> —Tessa Afshar, author and speaker

If you're a Mr. Rogers fan, you probably remember "Planet Purple," where all females are named Pauline and all males are Paul. They are all purple and all speak in the same monotone voice. When a Paul and a Pauline visited the Neighborhood of Make-Believe, they were shocked by the colors, emotions, and differences they discovered.

We think we want our men to be more like us. More our shade of purple. More sensitive, more intuitive, more in tune with our cadence of life. But do we? Do we really want our guys to be clones of our girlfriends? Sure, that would mean he might listen and intuit more, but we'd have to take the whole package. Including the drama!

About ten years ago, Cynthia and I spent an amazing couple

of days in Door County, the picturesque tip of Wisconsin's thumb. We were promoting *A Door County Christmas*, a novella collection we wrote with two author friends. I stopped for supper on my way home and just pulled back onto I-94, after dark, when something flashed in front of me. A deer, legs reaching wide in a graceful leap. As I slammed into it, things went flying. I was sure they were deer parts. I pulled to the side of the road, got out, breathed a sigh when I saw the grill and a headlight were missing and those were the parts I'd seen flying. Then I checked all my own body parts, decided I was fine, and did what any modern, independent woman would do. I called my husband.

To his credit, I think he asked if I was okay. Then he said, "Can you find the grill?" and "If you can find the deer, you can keep it."

Umm . . . Yep, hon, I'll get right on that.

I am five feet tall. But, hey, I am a woman. Hear me roar as I heft that carcass onto the top of my minivan.

To my credit, I did not start "intense fellowship." I said goodbye and ended the call. I looked for the deer and thankfully didn't find it. I cried a bit. And then I did what any modern, independent woman would do. I called a girlfriend.

"Oh, honey, are you okay?" Cynthia's voice on the other end was a balm to my soul. What a blessing to have a sympathetic sister to commiserate (and laugh hysterically) with.

But when I got home, it was my husband who diagnosed the hole in the radiator and fixed the tire that had miraculously let me drive more than seventy miles before going flat.

I need them both.

Vive la différence is a French phrase we've all heard. It literally translates as "long live the difference." Imagine doing a waltz with someone who took the exact same steps you did rather than stepping back with his right when you stepped forward with your left. The result would be a collision, and things would go flying. Long live the difference!

Choose a safe word or phrase that lets the other person know "I need time to process this, but I'm not ignoring you." It might be as simple as "Time-out" or "Gotta ponder" or "Pumpernickel." Or it could be more detailed. "I'm a visual learner. Let me sketch out what I think you're saying." Or, "Let me do some online research before we make a decision on that." If the phrase or wording is agreed upon ahead of time, and respectfully used, it can press pause on a disagreement that could otherwise escalate.

—Cynthia

CHAPTER 10

Are We Renting or Owning
This Marriage?

⸺ Cynthia ⸺

How invested are we when we're renting an apartment compared to when we own a house? A good renter takes care of minor repairs and upkeep, and, yes, sometimes that's simply so they can get their security deposit back when they move. Other renters trash the place with no regard for the owners or the structure itself.

Want to replace the front door with something more welcoming? Can't if you're renting. Looking to improve the traffic flow from kitchen to living room? Not only can you not do so without the landlord's or apartment manager's permission, but it would be a waste of time if you're just renting.

Looking to build equity that benefits you for the long haul? Renting isn't it.

Home ownership comes with a whole new set of opportunities, but also responsibilities and commitment.

We don't rent or rent to own a marriage. In theory, we take legal ownership from the moment we sign the license. Sometimes it requires a little more time for couples to take emotional and relational ownership. Sadly, some never do, treating their marriage as if it's a loaner vehicle.

Having survived life's other adjustments, couples often find that the inherent irritations and frustrations of a 24/7 spouse in the house send them back into renter mentality. Upkeep is someone else's responsibility, right?

Well . . . not really. You can't expect someone else to take responsibility for your leaky marriage faucet. It's time to own it. The responsibility for upkeep and repairs—especially during seasons of WHATT—lies on the shoulders of the husband and wife. And there are definitely benefits to owning your marriage. If you rent, you're limited in the changes you can make to a structure. If you own, you can decide to add on, replace what isn't working, or repurpose an unused spare bedroom into a refuge. It makes marriage ownership appealing, doesn't it?

Right now, my guy and I are together 24/7. We work side by side with our office chairs two feet from one another all day, every day. As you can imagine, this has taught me a lot:

1. He's even better at his job than I always imagined. He's an incredible manager for his team, leading them with compassion, fairness, humor, and encouragement through these unstable times while making unseen sacrifices to save other people's jobs.

2. He doesn't take his stress and anxiety out on me. Even when he's juggling a million balls and putting out fires by the minute, he'll still look over at me and smile or get up just to hug me or slip off to the kitchen to grab us a treat. He knows how to pocket his work stress in a place that doesn't hurt me. And I appreciate that so very much.

—Julie Cantrell, author of *Into the Free*
and *The Feathered Bone*

When you own your marriage, you get to ask the big questions: What's your goal for your marriage? What will it take to reach that goal?

As mentioned in an earlier chapter, one wise couple eventually "realized we wanted the same thing in our marriage—loving each other." Knowing your goal—to glorify God with your life as individuals and as a couple—can help establish boundaries, encourage problem-solving techniques, and change the atmosphere in a together-all-the-time home.

Marriage partners who own it, who step up to the plate to do whatever needs to be done to keep the relationship in good repair, and even more so in WHATT households, quickly learn several key life lessons:

- An unaddressed small problem will almost inevitably become a large and expensive one. A leaky water heater leads to a crumbling foundation; unresolved misunderstanding leads to a crumbling marriage.
- Your spouse's happiness is not your responsibility, but you do have influence over the atmosphere in which happiness can grow and thrive . . . or shrivel and die.
- If life's circumstances make the walls feel like they're closing in, don't look for the escape hatch. Knock down a wall. Establishing an open concept during a closed-in-together season (or lifetime!) may mean adding more support overhead, but it offers more breathing room.
- If an apartment isn't ideal, but you're renting, not owning, resentment builds against the landlord. If you're owning a marriage, resentment can build against each other, which destroys rather than fixes.
- No reconstruction or renovation comes without paying a price in inconvenience, messes, and a few blisters. End

result? So worth it at the reveal. And worth it from that day on.

If we're in this marriage for the long haul, we make decisions with that commitment in mind. Should we invest in this weekend project—a marriage retreat? How important will this seem in two months? In twenty years? Could it stop our foundation from crumbling?

Storm knocks the power out? The answer isn't moving. It's waiting for the power to be restored. And calling the divine Power Company.

Wise homeowners think ahead—installing security measures, replacing draft-prone windows, waterproofing basement walls, adding another layer of insulation in the attic to save on heating bills, and in some locations investing in hurricane shutters or earthquake-resistant stabilizers. They do so because they're committed. They care about what they're protecting in a much deeper way than a renter would.

And those who are in it for the long haul prepare well to weather whatever lies ahead.

Storm knocks the power out? The answer isn't moving. It's waiting for the power to be restored. And calling the divine Power Company.

— Becky —

Dr. Snuggles and I have signed dozens of lease agreements, some as tenants, some as landlords. The contracts we make with our renters are for a one-year lease with month-to-month rent after that. In that first year, if a tenant is not happy with their space (or us), they are obligated to keep paying rent until we find new renters, which usually happens within thirty days. If we are not pleased with their chronically late payments or destruction of property, we need to show just cause before evicting them. After that first year, either party can end the agreement with a thirty-day notice.

Signing a mortgage is different. We have had sleepless nights every time we signed a purchase agreement, even with our fifth house. We loved the property and were thrilled to be moving. But the commitment involved was scary.

Signing a marriage certificate should be a little scary too. There's no thirty-day-notice exit clause and you're solemnly agreeing to something that should last longer than a thirty-year mortgage.

Sadly, some of us walk down the aisle with an exit strategy tucked in our bouquets. I still cringe when I think of the words a good friend spoke on the eve of her wedding: "Well, if things don't work out, we can always get a divorce."

Merriam-Webster Online defines a *vow* as "a solemn promise or assertion; *specifically*: one by which a person is bound to an act, service, or condition."[1]

What pictures come to mind when you think of the word *bound*? At my granddaughter's beautiful outdoor wedding, she and her new husband handed out wide, colorful ribbons to all the children. Grasping each other's hands, the newlyweds invited the children to bind their hands together with the ribbons. It was a precious, symbolic, love-and-laughter-filled moment.

This centuries-old practice of "handfasting" is becoming popular again. I love the twist added by my granddaughter and grandson-in-law. By including family in this part of the ceremony, they not only acknowledged the foreverness of their pledge to each other but also recognized their need for the support of the people they had invited to witness the vows they made to each other before God.

The "before God" part is an important detail.

In traditional wedding vows, the officiant says, "_____, wilt thou have this woman/man to be thy wedded wife/husband, to live together after God's ordinance in the holy estate of matrimony? Wilt thou love her/him, comfort her/him, honor and keep her/him, in sickness and in health, and forsaking all others keep thee only unto her/him as long as you both shall live?"

The bride and groom take turns saying, "I will," then move on to, "In the name of God, I, _____, take you, _____, to be my wife/husband, to have and to hold from this day forward, for better, for worse, for richer, for poorer, in sickness and health, to love and to cherish, until we are parted by death. This is my solemn vow."

Most of us, no matter how old we are when we marry, are woefully clueless about the many layers hidden beneath "for better, for worse" and "as long as you both shall live." We are, and should be, starry-eyed and certain we are venturing forth into a gloriously happy "ever after."

> Most of us, no matter how old we are when we marry, are woefully clueless about the many layers hidden beneath "for better, for worse" and "as long as you both shall live."

I remember growing absolutely giddy over picturing our toothbrushes hanging side by side. Remember being there? When the thought of saying "Good night" instead of "Good-bye" at the end of the day filled you with rapture? When you couldn't imagine ever getting to the point where you'd *want* to say "Good-bye" instead of "Good night" at 10 p.m.?

And yet . . . here you are, sharing air with this person who once made your toes tingle, but now it's your fingertips tingling from lack of oxygen.

Maybe you wrote your own vows. We used the traditional "in sickness and in health" part, then added our own words.

My almost husband said: "In taking you as my wife, I promise to accept you as you are, and to love and cherish you above all else, in all times and circumstances, and to do the best I can to help make this a still better and more fulfilling relationship in the time ahead."

I replied, "In taking you as my husband, I accept your weaknesses as well as your strengths. I give myself, not only as your wife but as your constant friend. I promise to hold out my hand when you are lonely, to be a quiet listener when you need to talk, and to always be at your side when you need support."

Ouch. That word "always" in the last sentence was hyperbole, right? And "I promise" really meant "I'll give it my best shot," didn't it?

I have definitely aced the "accept your weaknesses" clause. Because, of course, "accept" doesn't mean leaving it up to God to change anything that needs to be changed. It means, "I vow to point out your weaknesses and give you frequent suggestions about what you can do to improve them, and I promise to gift you with daily pointers on how you can start doing things the right, aka *my*, way." (*Cynthia here. Chortling. The perfect spot for chortling.*)

Years ago, when I couldn't find my copy of our vows, I wrote to the pastor who married us. The letter that accompanied the copy he sent me, written on church stationary and dated three days before our seventh anniversary, says, "You are fortunate to be able to get this, since our parsonage was gutted by fire while we were on vacation."

Wow. The vows we had made before God were almost destroyed by fire "while we were on vacation." So much dual meaning in that opening sentence. Before our seventh anniversary, I'd had moments of forgetting my promises, of mentally packing up my commitment and heading off on vacation. Our vows could have been gutted by fire.

Have you been there? Are you there now? What's creating that selective amnesia that's tempting you to turn your back on your promise to God and the person you wanted to do ever after with? Boredom? Neglect? Misunderstandings? Someone else looks better, listens more? Close proximity seems more suffocating than comforting?

British American author and speaker Jill Briscoe tells about a time when she was teaching about David and Bathsheba at a women's conference. Rather than going to war, fighting God's battles with his men, King David found himself on a rooftop watching a beautiful young woman bathe. He sent for her, messengers brought her to the palace, and the king's lustful choices sparked a firestorm of sad consequences.

When Jill finished her talk, a woman approached her and said, "I just don't relate to this, Jill. My husband is a pastor. We have a wonderful marriage and family and a great church. I would never commit adultery."

Jill responded, "Have you ever had the chance?"

When the woman said she had been approached once, then described the rather unattractive man, Jill warned, "It's easy to say no to a King Lear type, but it will be more difficult if a King David moves in next door!"

Years later, Jill received a frantic note from that woman, pleading, "Pray for me, Jill. King David moved in next door."

Sadly, the woman did not listen to Jill's advice. Her choice destroyed her marriage.[2]

As Cynthia likes to say, marriages never implode without help from the humans tending them.

If for any reason you're tempted to turn your back on the vows you made before God, please confess to Him what He already knows, then find a trusted friend or counselor.

Sometimes what's needed is stepping away from the marriage for a predetermined season while you both remain faithful to each other and seek wise counsel. Sometimes there are biblical grounds for walking away (see the appendixes in the back). But often we can find our way back to what we once had if we start with a reminder of the solemn promise we made before God . . . which can only be kept with His minute-by-minute help. And this is supported by research—the vast majority of people surveyed who considered their marriage unhappy considered themselves happy five years later.[3] Marriage isn't for rent.

Scripture doesn't tell us exactly what happened in David's heart, the excuses he made for himself, or the gratification he felt he deserved, but we do know our own weaknesses and vulnerabilities. Even though we've signed those mortgage papers with every intention of being faithful to that promise, it just might be smart to stay off the roof.

CHAPTER 11

Money Talks, but It's Not Telling My Spouse What It's Telling Me

— Cynthia —

He's worked hard for decades. Now it's time to play, he says. "Let's go boat shopping!"

You've worked hard for decades. Now it's time to downsize, tighten those belts, and learn to be content with less. "Let's put the house on the market and sell one vehicle."

Home-based entrepreneurs who are both marriage *and* business partners might differ wildly in their attitudes about profit and loss, investing in inventory, or spending the kids' college funds to build the company.

Maybe one spouse made an unwise expenditure or two, and now you're both paying the consequences. And the non-spender won't let the spender forget it.

How does a couple—any couple, but especially spouses living long hours in the same house—deal with financial regret or polar opposite opinions about money? Times of forced confinement such as retirement, both spouses working from home, layoffs, and short-term or long-term illness often escalate the potential for financial disagreements. Couples begin to notice each other's money quirks—or downright weirdness—up close and personal.

Finances might be especially tight because of the business or lack of it, or the economy, or because one partner is more skilled at shopping online and the newly at-home spouse is hawkeyed when packages arrive on the doorstep.

Ordinary life already gives a billion reasons for a couple to disagree about money matters. Spending issues can affect our perspective until that SITH—spouse in the house—morphs into something more like the Star Wars villain version rather than our partner. The simple fact is that the spouse in your house has a high probability of thinking differently than you do about pinching pennies or throwing them in wishing wells.

It's not that I wasn't forewarned my mate and I were wired and raised differently regarding money matters. (And they do matter.) I found it charming that Wonderhubby was so careful with money and that he thought as young marrieds we could each survive on ten dollars for an allowance for two weeks, which was less than a sixth grader made at the time.

No, I didn't find it charming. Not charming at all.

I did appreciate that he was careful. I did not appreciate that he expected me to outdo him in the frugal department.

I was raised in a household that was not rich, or even well-off actually, but one marked by generosity to a fault. I considered (still do) generosity one way of expressing the extravagant love of God. Wonderhubby now agrees, but as we've worked to compromise and respect each other's opinions, I've converted to valuing his thoughtfulness and wisdom with finances. Most of the time. Except when he says, "We need to talk." Becky will share more on that in a moment.

One thing we've learned is that if money becomes anything other than provision we are grateful for and steward well, it has unnecessarily become a point of contention. Good bomb sniffers will recognize the odor of explosive attitudes regarding financial concerns.

When is money something other than provision?

- *When it becomes an idol*—either the saving of it or the spending of it. If money pulls our thoughts away from where they should be focused, it's getting too much attention. If its accumulation makes decisions for us, we've lost our perspective on its role. If bowing to wealth's or poverty's demands means money is a hot topic in your home, it's become a ruling party. A dictator rather than a tool like any other we use in life.
- *When it becomes a threat.* "He didn't even notice I went out of my way to make his favorite meal tonight. That stings. Let's see how he feels if I spend a little time shopping online tonight. I bet he notices that."
- *When it shoves us into a competitive battle.* "You'll notice I spent more money for your birthday than you did for mine, honey." "Not if you count shipping and handling. That makes me three dollars ahead of you in gift giving."
- *When it becomes a battering ram.* "You're going to have to contribute more to our financial picture. No way around it now." "Really? As hard as I've worked, you're telling me it's not enough?"
- *When it is marked by love or lust.* The Bible is often misquoted as saying money is evil, a distortion of 1 Timothy 6:10. What it really says is that if money becomes the thing we long for, lust after, will walk over even our spouse to get, or possessively hide from our spouse, it has morphed from a cultural necessity to a passion bordering on obsession. And *that's* evil.

> **Does the specter of money issues sleep between you at night? Declare the bedroom off-limits to financial discussions or concerns.**

- *When it plays a role belonging to God.* Is money or your income itself your provision? No. It's evidence of God's provision. Is money your security? No, He is. Is money your problem solver? No. Again, it's God.
- *When it comes between you.* "There are three of us on the couch, in the car, even in our bed—him, me, and his concern about money hogging the space between us." In your household, it may be that the woman is the more frugal or anxiety-ridden about finances. In few households do both parties think exactly the same about finances, which can offer its own dangers. Rarely does perpetual peace reign regarding money issues. But when it wedges in between us, it's no longer a financial issue. It's become a marriage pinch point. Does the specter of money issues sleep between you at night? Declare the bedroom off-limits to financial discussions or concerns.

How do WHATT couples handle differing perspectives on this complicated but necessary subject? Applicable for any season of marriage, but all the more important during together-all-the-time—when we notice every flaw or conflict like dust motes in bright sunlight—are these tips.

Find Common Ground

What do you agree on? Living debt free? Giving to God first? Using thoughtfulness rather than thoughtlessness—intentionality rather than impulse—as a financial decision maker? Once you've identified it, celebrate the common ground you share.

Discover and Capitalize on Your Strengths

Wonderhubby feels responsible for and comfortable with managing our family finances, as long as it doesn't involve technology. But he gets hives thinking about the complexities of my self-employment finances, so we've agreed that he handles that side and I handle this side. I prepare the self-employment info when it comes to tax time, and he compiles the rest.

We talk often about where we stand and are willing and ready to make adjustments as needed. I'm not married to a preconceived notion about who should make payments or go to the bank or reconcile the bank statement. I'm married to Wonderhubby.

When income streams change radically, whatever the reason, capitalizing on each other's strengths will help a couple negotiate and renegotiate monetary peace.

Make Life Easier for the Spouse with the Opposite Viewpoint

Now there's a concept. We can make life rougher, intentionally or unintentionally, when we make purchasing demands of a provider-mentality spouse who feels the most responsible to keep the family afloat financially, or who *is* the primary income earner, or who feels a God-given call to manage the household's finances. And conversely, we add to a generosity-fueled spouse's concerns if we don't consider that drive or sense of responsibility legitimate.

In a WHATT household, adjustments abound. If wisdom also abounds, we'll do everything in our scope to ease the jolt of those adjustments rather than escalating their impact.

Early in our marriage, I discovered that if I whined about what we couldn't have, it didn't change anything except for making my husband feel worse. And he soon discovered that if he responded to every request or question with "We can't afford it," something in me felt as if my request wasn't taken seriously or that he saw me, rightly or wrongly, as That Woman Who Costs Me Money.

When instead he began to respond with a small but meaningful adjustment to his dialogue—"I wish we could afford that right now"—I felt acknowledged even if the end result was a no.

A wise counselor once said, "Ask yourself, 'What does this make possible?'" It can be applied to any number of small and large decisions.

If I spend this money, what does it make possible? Not much good. The item that caught my fancy will disappear before I know it. But it might make possible that I don't have enough for the important item I'll need next month.

If I gripe to my mate about the money he spent on that new putter, what does that make possible? He will feel guilty instead of grateful every time he golfs with it. It could make a breach, even temporarily, in our relationship. The right decision may be not to gripe, but to be grateful he has a hobby he enjoys, and that he didn't decide his choice of hobby was *me*. The exception, of course, is if either party is spending unwisely and creating financial distress or strain. That may need an expert to help untangle.

Money may talk, as they say. And it practically shouts when we find ourselves in a different financial picture due to retirement, restructuring, job loss, or whatever it is that creates your two-spouses-in-the-house situation. But when it talks, it's time to listen . . . to each other, to God's biblical principles regarding money, and maybe even to a financial planner who has our interests at heart but can advise us without partiality, past regrets, our disagreement history, and that third entity on the couch or in the car getting between us.

—— **Becky** ——

Every marriage has trigger words—those syllables that, when strung together by your SITH, create instant dread. Or, in my case, full-out panic. Words like *budget meeting*. Or "We need to talk" (spoken with the credit card bill or grocery receipt in hand).

When a woman says, "We need to talk," a man feels like she's just lined up all her cannons.

—Duane H.

Anyone else's hands sweating? Knees knocking? What excuses jump in to rescue you from what will, beyond the shadow of doubt, turn into one of the most intense "fellowships" you've ever had?

Dr. Snuggles is the money person in our family. It only makes sense. He's a business owner. He's left-brained. He's linear and logical and practical. I am not any of those things. Remember the carefree, barefoot poet person? Yeah. Put me in charge of our finances and we'll both be barefoot. And *bare*ly speaking.

According to a budgeting personality quiz developed by Dave Ramsey, founder of Financial Peace University, Dr. Snuggles is a nerd and I'm a free spirit. Nerds enjoy creating budgets and calculating numbers. It gives them a sense of security. Free spirits want nothing to do with crunching numbers and tend to forget about budgets. Free spirits may feel controlled or not cared for by their nerdy spouses, while nerds may view free spirits as irresponsible.

It's rare for two people who deeply love each other to be perfectly synced in their love of handling (or even discussing) a budget. What if one of you wants to pinch pennies so your kids will get a substantial inheritance while the other wants to live large in the eat-drink-and-be-merry moment? What if he decides, now that you're both home all the time and can work from anywhere, that it's time to sell the house and buy a fifth wheel or a sailboat . . . or a live-in food truck? (I made that up. Live-in food trucks probably create health-code violations.)

What if, now that you're staring at that old vinyl flooring sixteen hours a day, you figure it's time to replace it? But the logical thing to do is to start at the top and work down. New cupboards, countertops, appliances, island . . . You're asking friends for recommendations on who to hire, and all the while he's adding shelves and tool bins to his Amazon wish list while mapping out his new workshop. And there's no room in the budget for both. It's enough to make a girl grind her teeth and resort to muttering about joining the HHATT Club.

Whether you're dealing with ample resources or disagreeing on how to spend the change found under the couch cushions, there will be friction. Oh, speaking of change . . . a friend just told me that when he wants to make a purchase he knows his budget-handler wife won't approve of, he simply dips into his hidden stash of over a thousand dollars in "spare" change. I'm picturing hollowed-out books, socks full of pennies, false-bottom desk drawers, and a very lumpy mattress!

That could work. So could separate checking accounts. "Your paycheck goes in yours, and I'll keep mine, thank you. You pay the mortgage; I'll pay the utilities. We'll split groceries and gas, and whatever is left is our own fun money."

While separate accounts and secret funds might work, it's also possible these hacks could undermine the need for transparency—a key component in intimacy and living like you're in the WHATT Club together.

So what's the answer? Hang on while I grab a paper bag to breathe in.

It just may be that the peacekeeping answer is a (. . . *breeeathe* . . .) budget meeting.

There. That wasn't so bad. I've actually survived quite a few. Do I enjoy them? Forty-eight years in, and I'd still volunteer to walk on hot coals rather than schedule time with our financial advisor. (Are those hives on my neck?)

Not **talking about dreams, desires, priorities, and the reality of how much is actually in the checking account causes more problems than the momentary misery of pie charts and bar graphs.**

But what I've come to realize is that *not* talking about dreams, desires, priorities, and the reality of how much is actually in the checking account causes more problems than the momentary misery of pie charts and bar graphs.

All wise financial advisors' guidelines for budget *talks* (so much softer than "meetings," isn't it?) include planning ahead to avoid the deer-in-the-headlights effect of those five little words, "We need to talk *now*." They also recommend agreeing on a time limit and showing up prepared. Dave Ramsey also suggests bringing chocolate to the table. That last one is key. How intensely can you argue while munching on Toll House cookies warm from the oven? Melted chocolate chips cover a multitude of unwise spending.

I'd also add: Start by praying together, and read Philippians 2:3–4 out loud. "Do nothing out of selfish ambition or vain conceit. Rather, in humility value others above yourselves, not looking to your own interests but each of you to the interests of the others."

If you think of this as a time to bless your spouse by listening to his hopes and aspirations and helping to find a way to realize those dreams, and if he's thinking the same for you, it's not likely the *talk* will derail.

This is also an opportunity to practice the gift of self-sacrifice. He really, really wants that workshop. You really, really want that new kitchen. Can you modify your vision, or maybe postpone it? Could that workshop include space and tools to cut the new tiles and sand the old cupboards?

If we arrive at our kitchen table budget meeting armed with pen and paper, chocolate, an open mind, and a willing heart, remembering that we're on the same team and in this for good and forever, even a nerd and a free spirit can walk hand in hand into a planning talk for a happy-as-we-can-make-it-ever-after future.

CHAPTER 12

Get That Out of My Pail! (His Bucket List Doesn't Play Well with Mine)

— Becky —

If you dream of planting yourself in a beach chair and taking root in the sand, but he has visions of the two of you renting Harleys and spending weeks whipping around the sharp hairpin bends of the steepest mountainside roads in Northern Europe, you've got a problem. But keeping your bucket list dreams without destroying his might not be as difficult as you think.

One of my daughters-in-law recently wrote a blog post titled "Filling the Bucket . . ."[1] A decade ago, while homeschooling our three oldest grandchildren, she gave the kids the assignment of creating a bucket list. (The term once referred to "things I'd like to do before I die" but has now come to mean "things I'd like to do while I live" or even just "dreaming.") While the kids worked on their lists, my daughter-in-law made one for herself. The things on her list ranged from small and doable (#3 Find a piece of sea glass) to huge and maybe impossible (#25 Fly over a volcano in a helicopter).

Dr. Snuggles and I have accomplished many items on our own bucket lists—backpacking in the mountains, buying a motorcycle, zip-lining, kayaking—but we continue to add more.

I don't want to leave this world with everything crossed off. If God keeps us here until we're 120, I hope we're still dreaming about our next adventure (even if it's winning at wheelchair races or the next game of bingo).

Do you have a bucket list? If not, consider putting a bookmark in this page and picking up a pen and paper or clicking to a new document. Take a moment to savor the expanse of white. A blank slate inviting you to dream. If you feel intimidated, start small. What would you love to do on Saturday? On your next birthday? What do you want to make or learn or watch? What new doors to adventure are open now that you're both home together? Midweek camping or picnics, late-night stargazing, work-on-the-road trips?

Stifle the little voice telling you it's too expensive, you'll never have the time, you're not smart enough, you're too old, too young, or not being practical. Let your dreams flow until they fill the page.

Now, hand your spouse a pen and paper and ask him to do the same. No restrictions. Tell him they can be things he'd like to do with or without you. Let him know he's not allowed to take cost into consideration. When he's done, talk about the ones you want to share. (It's okay to have a separate list titled "Too Wild and Crazy to Tell Anyone but God.")

Wouldn't this be a great date night activity? Over dinner, or while taking a walk, talk about your "Someday . . ." lists. You may be surprised to discover you'd both like to learn to play the ukulele or spend a night in an ice hotel.

Your hubby's list is a treasure trove of romantic gift ideas. Dr. Snuggles occasionally mentioned it would be fun to try flying a small plane, so one year I gave him a discovery flight gift card for Christmas. He enjoyed it so much he signed up for lessons and got his private pilot license. Not what I had in mind, because, though I love flying—in great big sturdy commercial jets where the pilot wears a spiffy uniform and you've never seen him drive through a red light because he wasn't paying attention—this was different.

> The smartest thing we did for our relationship [when we entered a season of 24/7 togetherness] was keeping date night alive. It was sometimes drive-through coffee or dinner in the car. The conversations kept us encouraged and realigned with one another. The smartest thing we did for our home during that time was that we made it an adventure. We bought lots of board games, tried new recipes, and went for family hikes as much as we could.
>
> —Derrick Williams, assistant pastor at Emmanuel
> Baptist Church, Newington, Connecticut

For months, I refused to go up with him, even though he assured me there were no stoplights to miss up there and a Cessna 150 is really just a glider that can land easily even if the engine quits. (*Even if the engine quits?*) When I finally mustered the courage, I absolutely loved it. His dream became mine.

A few years ago, Dr. Snuggles and I started a corny-sounding birthday tradition. On his birthday, he gets a Prince Day. Thirteen days later, I get a Princess Day. Every year we give each other a choice: "Do you want to choose what you do and how you spend the day, or be surprised?" My choice usually involves dropping enough hints that I get a bit of both. And I love surprising him. It helps if I take notes when a friend mentions a unique restaurant or a great movie that piques his interest. One of the perks of being home together is that we actually get to celebrate *on* our birthdays rather than waiting for a free weekend.

This takes us right back to Philippians 2:4 and Paul's encouragement to look to the interests of others. Let's talk about your spouse's bucket-list dreams that didn't take you by surprise. The ones you've known about for years and just ignored because . . .

well, maybe you've seen him run stoplights and weren't sure you could trust his attentiveness at eight thousand feet above terra firma. Is there a way to compromise? Can you give it a try? Or be the cheerleader on the ground taking a video of his first solo flight?

Maybe the thought of getting your motorcycle license terrifies you. I get that. I took two lessons and decided it wasn't for me. Yep, I'm a wimp, but I love riding on the back of our Gold Wing bike. Could you join your man on his motorcycle at low elevations, then give him the freedom to explore sheer-drop fjord roads on his own while you sit by the fireplace sipping hot, rich *turkaffe* at the historic mountaintop Stalheim Hotel in Norway? Not a bad compromise.

But what about the things on your list that make him wrinkle his nose? A little give-and-take goes a long way. "We could spend an hour at the craft fair and then have lunch at that burger place you love."

And what about asking God—together—what *He's* put on your bucket lists? That zip line experience I mentioned flew us a hundred feet over a jungle in Belize. We were there on a mission trip—something God put on our lists. Don't be surprised if He adds a whole new column.

> **What about asking God—together—what *He's* put on your bucket lists?**

Number twenty-five on my daughter-in-law's list? My sweet granddaughter blessed her with a fiftieth birthday trip to Hawaii that included a helicopter ride over a volcano. The last line in her "Filling the Bucket . . ." blog post recommends sharing your list because, "After all, you never know what—or who—might help make your dream come true."[2]

⟶ Cynthia ⟶

I'll never forget the day Wonderhubby leaned forward and said, "Hey! You work from home. And I'm retiring soon. You could work from anywhere!"

My heart beat faster. After all these years, was it possible? We could move to a warmer climate? Provide a great vacation spot for our kids and grandkids to come enjoy the beach? My breath caught in my throat as I thought of a longer growing season for garden vegetables, fresh fruit year-round, sunshine as an expectation rather than a curiosity, winters with no below-zero temperatures and no need to even own a winter coat, boots, and thermal mittens!

"Yes, hon, it's true. As long as I have internet, I can work from anywhere. We're free to move somewhere else." The Caribbean? No, he'd think that was extreme. Florida? No, the tourism wasn't a draw for him. Arizona? Maybe. I waited for him to ask if I'd do an online search for inexpensive tropical locations in which to retire.

He said, "As long as it's no farther south."

What? He wanted to move farther *north*? That was *not* on my bucket list.

The "else" of "somewhere else" meant some place other than our home in the heart of Wisconsin, where a "cold snap" could last from October to May, temps dip to thirty or forty below zero for a week or more at a time, and the short growing season is often interrupted by an early frost.

To date, it's the last time we brought up the subject. Peace is on *my* bucket list, so . . .

I love to travel. Wonderhubby likes to see the sights when we're there, but he doesn't enjoy what it takes to get there. I could sit on an ocean beach for hours, staring at the water, filling my soul with all good things. After a few minutes on the beach, he's ready to leave. "Come on, let's go. We saw it."

I'd like to take in the ancient architecture of Europe. He'd like to see the ruins of a Yukon explorer's cabin. He dreams of slowing life down and breathing his last breath while fishing. My idea of slowing down involves a cleaning lady and a hired cook, and I dream of hearing the call to Glory and asking, "Can I finish this one last sentence first?"

If I call my personal chef a nutritionist, is it covered by Medicare?

Last night, I finished kitchen cleanup and took my tea to the family room, where Wonderhubby was watching TV. I know. Shocking. He said, "I don't think you'd like this movie."

"What is it?"

"*Tarzan.*"

Great. But wait. The scene showed a young man in an ascot. He and his wife were dressed impeccably and lived in a well-appointed manor in Victorian England. Did you know the difference between a manor and a mansion is how much land the estate includes? I guess it was a mansion, then.

Brocade fabric on the walls. Intricately carved woodwork. Interesting characters and relationship dynamics. Maybe I'd stay and watch a few minutes.

I enjoyed every minute of the movie, including the fight scenes and the explosions, because it unfolded as characters with backstory fought their pasts to move forward into an unknown but dangerous future.

Whether we're talking about big bucket-list ideas or simple daily pleasures, we won't know what's on our spouse's list if we don't ask and, conversely, if we don't share ours.

What do you know? A movie we could both appreciate. He may have listed the chase scenes and hand-to-hand combat as his reasons for enjoying *The Legend of Tarzan*. I may have listed the scenery, the human drama, the angst, the longing. It didn't matter that our reasons were different.

If he'd insisted I watch the movie with him, if he'd jotted his own notes on my schedule or my bucket list, the chase scenes and explosions might have bothered me. But he didn't need to know I was focused on the costuming, the dynamics between characters, the deeper meaning behind each action, the way the sun's shadows played on the jungle floor.

Whether we're talking about big bucket-list ideas or simple daily pleasures, we won't know what's on our spouse's list if we don't ask and, conversely, if we don't share ours. Consider making a simple-pleasures list for your spouse.

I feel closest to you and want you closest to me:

- When you come up behind me in the kitchen to give me an unexpected hug, kiss the back of my neck, or ask, "Can I help with something?"
- When you say, "Can we pray together?"
- When you bring me a flower (or flowers) just because
- When you choose being with me above being with the television
- When you read a book or watch a video about improving our relationship

What do you imagine would be on your spouse's list? Ask!

Wilderness adventures are my husband's cup of t— No. I'm a tea snob married to someone who dislikes—*dislikes*, mind you—tea and coffee. He enjoys wilderness adventures. And I accompanied him on a few.

One night when we were tenting on a granite island (not the kitchen kind, the landmass kind) in the middle of a Canadian lake miles from civilization, he woke me at two in the morning. "You gotta see this," he said.

I see very little at two in the morning. But I did note that the tent was engulfed in darkness. If he'd found an interesting pinecone or something, he might regret waking me for that.

"Come on," he said, holding the tent flap open for me. The gentleman.

Because of the absence of light pollution from even our single yard light at home, the stars shone as bright as I'd ever seen them. I could see deeper into the night sky than ever before.

And he didn't want me to miss it. Or the way the still lake mirrored every single star.

When I spent a month in Copenhagen, in the heart of the city, he was content to relive it with me later through pictures and stories. We plan our autumn getaways and vacations around spots of interest to both of us. I no longer sleep in tents on rocks. We've learned how to invite each other to appreciate our bucket lists vicariously but not to create the other person's list.

He already knows I'm not going skydiving. Ever. And it's not because I'm being stubborn about it. It's because I have an insatiable appetite for life, and I can't satisfy that appetite if I'm a parachute-draped pancake lying in a pile of myself.

It's okay with me if I need to listen to bassoon concertos with my headphones if he's home. I don't mind.

But if he insists we move farther north . . .

A wise sage once advised, "Let there be spaces in your togetherness." When a couple is newly married, one spouse might assume they will do nearly everything in tandem.

However, happy marriages benefit from both individual and shared activities. In our marriage of nearly forty-five years, my husband and I have pursued separate hobbies and avocations that have enriched our shared lives. I love theatre; he loves sports. He volunteers as a coach; I teach a Bible study. The time apart allows for personality differences and activity preferences, and our union is the better for it.

—Maggie Wallem Rowe, author of *This Life We Share*

CHAPTER 13

It's Still My Rib, Adam.
It's Still My Rib Cage, Eve.

— Cynthia —

It's my rib, Adam. And my rib and I would like to go to my pedicure by myself, okay?

You've been looking forward to this day for years. Your time is finally your own. No boss hovering over your shoulder, no kids demanding attention. You can do what you want . . . until you discover he's been longing for this day too, when you can finally be together 24/7, joined at the hip in wedded bliss, never out of each other's sight.

And what about when it's business, which in turn means your household income, that keeps both spouses at home? A cottage industry? A farm family? Two work-from-home adults in the house? Shared office space? Entrepreneurial endeavors where one spouse is the boss and the other the only employee, or perhaps both are co-owners?

Or what if a deployed spouse is finally home, but hurting? Or having a hard time reentering the workforce and just wants to be with you?

Remember the song with the lyrics that in essence proclaimed the person "couldn't live" if living was without her? She was either his girlfriend at the time or the woman he met earlier that day. Not sure. Sounds romantic, doesn't it?[1]

Sounds *melodra-mantic*. And unhealthy.

It might make for evocative songwriting or appeal to the all-in-ness of true love, but it sounds more Romeo-and-Juliet-foolish than romantic for the long haul.

Side note: In unrelated incidents eight years apart, both of the song's creators committed suicide. That doesn't say anything directly about the song, but it might speak to the idea that if we literally can't survive without our spouse, how emotionally stable are we?

A few years ago, I watched a young unmarried couple with interest. I knew they were in trouble when I noticed the young woman could not stand to be more than a few inches away from him. She draped herself over him when they sat side by side on the couch. She leaned her head on his shoulder in restaurants and clung to his upper arm with both hands. If he stood to move to another room, so did she. If he walked outside, she asked, "Where are you going?"

And she could not believe he was being truthful with her when he said where he'd been when they were apart for a day.

Any relationship built on fear of being apart hasn't fully matured, no matter how old it is.

Closeness? Good. Fear-filled dependence? Unhealthy.

Shared activities? Good. No activities that support the individuals' interests and an unwillingness to—or fear that one literally can't—survive without the other? Unhealthy.

Any relationship built on fear of being apart hasn't fully matured, no matter how old it is. Or it's based on underlying emotional issues that may be very real but are less than God's best.

Can we carve out individual space without leaving surgical scars? It starts with gratitude for a mate who loves being with you, then choosing your words wisely. Your need to be alone or with friends doesn't mean your spouse isn't enough for you or that you don't also enjoy togetherness time.

> There is a saying that goes something like this: "How can I miss you if you never leave?" My wife and I enjoy being together, but I am not the easiest person to live with. I have found that when we do some things separately, it is better. I have some hobbies like running, biking, and kayaking that she would prefer to skip. These hobbies tend to be a good distraction in times of turmoil. They force me to get out, enjoy the world around me, and think about what a truly wonderful, loving wife I have been blessed with.
>
> —Bruce B.

It's a sign of a healthy relationship.

One survival tip for times when life's circumstances have us in very close proximity for extended periods of time is to allow each other to be who we are. Is a married couple "one flesh" as the Bible describes it (Genesis 2:24)? Yes. Does that mean if I eat a cookie, Wonderhubby's blood sugar spikes? If I get a splinter, his finger hurts? (I had a bathroom example to use here, but I'll leave that to your imagination.)

We remain individuals, even though we're one flesh. It's not the only dichotomy in God's divine plan. When we grow as individuals, it benefits our relationship together. When we experience adventures on our own, the storytelling is richer when we come back together. When we add to our collection of conversations individually, we have a greater pool of insights corporately.

The couples with hobbies they share and hobbies they don't

share have a richer life experience than those who believe growing as individuals somehow hurts their togetherness.

It took a few years of my being on the road—or in the air— the equivalent of one week a month during the busy business and speaking season for my husband to stop singing "Ain't No Sunshine When She's Gone." My job required the travel. And it was hard work. The prep. The flights, canceled flights, rerouted flights, and delays. The responsibilities. The exhaustion and catch-up when I got home. I can list how many states I've visited, how many fascinating places I've been. But I usually saw the airport, the Uber, the conference center or hotel, and then the Uber and airport again. That's how I crisscrossed the country to amazing cities with noteworthy landmarks I didn't see.

To my husband, I'm sure it must have felt as if I enjoyed ten or twelve weeks of vacation a year. I was absent. Deep inside, he knew I was working, but what registered more profoundly was that I wasn't there. With him.

Sweet, right? Until it wasn't. I fought guilt over being gone, but I had no doubt it was God who orchestrated the opportunities. Who would I please? The God who called me or the man I loved? An impossible conundrum. My husband took several short fishing trips a year, but, in his words, "That's different."

Sometimes with tears, I offered to lay it all down if that's what my husband wanted me to do. But those conversations always ended with his acknowledging that the work I was doing was important, and that he didn't want to stand in God's way. He didn't want to accompany me, though I often offered. Big cities hold no appeal to him. Conferences? Torture chambers for him. When my destination was a spot that interested him, and we could afford it, we enjoyed a few extra days of mini vacation before or after a speaking event or conference. But it wasn't often we could swing his airfare plus a rental car.

Just when I thought there might be no solution but for me

to stop traveling, which I loved except for feeling guilty about contributing to my husband's loneliness, I overheard him tell someone, "Yes, she's gone a lot. I'm so proud of her and the work she does. Do I miss her? Sure. But I'm getting used to it. And actually, I'm finding things to do while she's gone. I look around for someone I can help, or hang out with the grandkids, or go to a movie I know she wouldn't appreciate. Also, I can have KFC or pizza every night if I want to."

He found a handyman's small group to attend. And he's exploring more local fishing spots.

It took awhile, but we're working it out. And I'm still willing to lay it all down for the sake of our marriage, if necessary. But I'm glad it isn't. The work is exhausting, yes, but deeply rewarding.

I haven't packed my bags in a few months now. He's starting to look at me like, "Don't you have somewhere you need to go?"

— Becky —

There's a reason why most romance novels or movies end before the honeymoon ends. Up until that point, the hero's and heroine's every waking moment is focused on the quest for ever-after togetherness. Every heartbeat pulses to the rhythm of "When Will I See You Again?"

And then they say "I do" and "I will" and they are . . . together forever. And things change. The romance doesn't go away, but it morphs into something that looks different. Where once we watched two individuals with separate lives living in breathless anticipation of never having to say good-bye, if they were still on the page or screen, we might just find two still-in-love, together-forever people wondering who they are now that they're half of a one-flesh whole, and what happened to the "me" part of life anyway?

Not so interesting to watch or read, but absolutely normal

and healthy. It takes awhile to reconfigure our identities when we enter into a life where every decision about how we'll spend our time or money should be made with a WHATT mindset. And if, a ways down the road, we find ourselves together for even more time, we need to do some more recalculating.

This is a good thing, a wonderful opportunity for self-discovery, but it can also go very wrong.

Know any chameleons? The friend who wants so desperately to keep the love alive that she changes her colors to meld with his? In her single life she enjoyed opera, ballet, and classical music, but when she fell for the shaggy-haired bass player in a grunge band, she traded her toe shoes for combat boots and claimed to prefer distorted electric guitar music over the Bach and Mozart that once flowed through her headphones and her veins. Because of their insecurity, these chameleons are closely related to the clingers Cynthia described.

While chameleons in the wild can change color to blend with their surroundings, they also change for other reasons. A female Madagascar chameleon who is not interested in mating may turn neon orange to scare the male away.

Similar characteristics can also be found in the human species. Some of us are so afraid of losing our identities that we'll do anything to keep from toning our unique, vibrant hues to shades that coordinate with his. ("I don't care what you want. I happen to like stone-hard butter!") This isn't a trait only reserved for females. An angered male chameleon may sport vivid multicolored stripes by way of warning. A human male may show his anger in more subtle ways. Like refusing to wash that lucky football jersey his mate claims is smelling up the closet.

Even though the intensely purple paisley couch our Hallmark heroine had in her studio apartment clashes with the hero's red plaid recliner, neither wants to give up these symbols of who they are. The husband who played sheepshead during every lunch hour before retirement may want to continue meeting his card buddies for a game every day. The wife who invited all the neighbor kids to bake cookies every Wednesday after school may want to continue the tradition even though that's now the time slot for her hubby's Zoom call with foreign investors.

What I call maintaining my identity might look like rejection to my spouse.

In my case, the fear of losing my free spirit (sometimes a euphemism for lack of discipline) to the mundane duties of being a wife, though irrational, was a problem. Would I become one of "those" women who only talked about recipes and new ways to remove ketchup stains from tablecloths?

> **What I call maintaining my identity might look like rejection to my spouse.**

I did eventually realize I could keep house, grocery shop, and care for a husband and children while still finding time to read, write, and grow as a person. But my fear sprang to life again when Dr. Snuggles started talking about retirement.

We were just kids, fifteen and sixteen, when we started dating. We spent every waking nonschool minute together. We walked to school hand in hand. He carried my books home. We studied together, ate supper at each other's houses, hung out on the weekends. (Cynthia here: Same for us, but we started even younger than that! Not recommended.) It was exhilarating. Until it wasn't. When my friends started planning things without me because I was always "with *him*." When assignments for my creative writing class got shoved to the last minute even though it used to be my favorite thing to do. When I started not knowing who I was without him.

I handled it like any mature seventeen-year-old. I broke up with him. Finally, I had my freedom. My time was my own. And I was miserable. I missed him. I had friends sneak photos of him on our class trip to Washington, DC, when I thought he wasn't looking. He *was* looking. Because he was miserable too. We did get back together, and the rest, as they say, is half a century of history, learning to be who God created us to be while still relishing being half of a one-flesh whole.

In my teens I didn't have the words to express needing alone time. All or nothing seemed to be the only answer. I've learned a few things since then, things I have to apply now that we're home together. All. The. Time:

- Who wants to be matchy-matchy? In college we had matching teal sweaters and gold corduroy bell-bottoms. It was fun, but if we did that all the time, we'd both suffocate. Different isn't bad. It's just different. He's logical and linear. I'm creative (read: *fly by the seat of my pants*). He's a runner. I prefer the slow movements of yoga. He's vitally interested in politics and current events. Just give me the headlines, please. Our quirks give us more to talk about.
- Eclectic is in, and not just when it comes to decor. With the right wallpaper and throw pillows, plaid and paisley can fit beautifully in the same room. With a bit of grace added, our opposites create a unique and pleasing color palette.
- Waving your colors too wildly can make your SITH wonder if you signed a declaration of independence along with your marriage license.
- We need balance. As Cynthia described, time apart makes us more interesting. But too much of it and, as Charles M. Schulz's character Charlie Brown says, "Absence makes the heart grow fonder, but it sure makes the rest of you lonely."

As I write this, a Shirley Novak poppy print hangs above my desk. Bright yellow, rose, tangerine, and vermilion blooms dance against a verdant background. Ms. Novak has painted hundreds of poppy pictures, each one unique. But imagine if she had only one paint color, if every blossom had to be the exact same shade of yellow. I'm guessing she would quickly grow tired of painting the same old flower. Without contrast, we bore easily. When our colors complement rather than clash, we can create a thing of beauty together.

CHAPTER 14

Why We Need HHATT Sisters and Guys Need Guy Friends

— Becky —

"There is a time for everything, and a season for every activity under the heavens" (Ecclesiastes 3:1).

The list that follows that verse includes a time to laugh, dance, weep, mourn, embrace, and speak. Those are all things we can do with our SITH, but, as we mentioned in the previous chapter, there are times (not whole seasons) when we need to do our own thing. We need occasions to laugh, weep, mourn, and speak to a BFF or a group of supportive girlfriends, and we need to encourage our men to connect with guy friends.

Did you know the myth that women speak twice as many words a day as men has been debunked? Researchers recorded the daily conversations of four hundred university students in the United States and Mexico over a period of several days. They found that females spoke about 16,215 words each day, and males uttered an average of 15,669 words, which was considered a statistical dead heat.[1]

However, one stereotype does seem to be backed by science: a statistically significant body of research has found that women are the more emotionally expressive gender in the realm of face-to-face communication. In general, we tend to display and talk about our feelings more than our men do.[2]

Women also tend to converse more about people, and men talk more about concrete concepts or objects.[3] No surprise there. Ask your man how he *feeeeels* about your relationship and you may hear crickets. (At least until he's had time to formulate an answer.) Ask him what he thinks about the national debt or the weird noise under the hood of the car, and you're more likely to get a plethora of immediate words.

Also not surprising is the fact that we generally like to listen to the same things we like to talk about. A few minutes into listening to my husband's thoughts on conspiracy theories or media bias, I feel my brain cells curling into fetal positions. Out of love for him, I'll engage for a while, but then I need to gently suggest he call a friend or one of our sons. I fully respect his need to talk and exchange mind-stimulating ideas. I need that as well . . . but on different topics.

I *need* my girlfriends. My husband needs me to need them too. I wasn't blessed with a biological sister, but I am so grateful for my circle of friends who listen, laugh, and pray for one another.

I'm part of a group of women that typically meets in a small upstairs room above our local coffeehouse. We call ourselves the Upper Room Ladies, or URL for short. We once decided to shake things up a bit for a Zoom meeting, so we all wore silly hats. The next week, we showed up with face paint. One sweet lady had a beautiful butterfly covering most of her face, painted by her very talented eleven-year-old grandson. Another sported a moustache. Laughter is good for the soul.

This group also created a "comfort bag." One of the women sewed a pretty cloth bag, and we took turns filling it with things that brought us comfort—books, tea, note cards, chocolate—adding an encouraging note, and delivering it to the front porch of the next person on the list. Second best thing to a hug!

In my stay-at-home-mom years, the phone was a lifeline. A call to Cathy or Judy could get me through a mountain of dishes or laundry. After those precious minutes of laughter and commiserating, I felt refreshed and ready to return to diapers and Lego-strewn floors and yet another call for mac and cheese. After God got hold of my heart, I found a new sanity saver—praying over the phone with a friend.

The book you are reading was birthed because two friends leaned on each other for sister support. It all started with conversations that boiled down to "He's home. All. The. Time."

"What now? How do I love and respect him when I can't stand the sound of his chewing?"

"This is the fourth bubble bath I've taken today, but I can't come up with another excuse to be alone that won't hurt his feelings. Help! I'm starting to look like a shar-pei!"

Those talks always ended with two things . . . laughter and prayer. Both are balms to a soul longing for some breathing room. Together, we worked on learning more God-honoring responses than the knee-jerk "Get out of my space!" We encouraged each other to look at a situation through our man's eyes. Iron sharpens iron, but the right friend can also act like a hot flat iron—smoothing, shaping, and calming flyaways.

> Iron sharpens iron, but the right friend can also act like a hot flat iron—smoothing, shaping, and calming flyaways.

Though science may have proven I don't actually have more words to use in a day than my husband, we're both grateful when some of my words get absorbed by girlfriends. If I'm talking to Cynthia, I know she'll be interested in the full, unabridged version of the server who took my order for gluten-free chicken and brought me a plate of something breaded with "just flour, no gluten." When I tell my husband, I'll give him a less detailed account. (A guy friend of ours is known for tipping his head and staring at his wife with glazed eyes before muttering, "Honey, does this story have a beginning, middle, and end?")

I'm equally grateful when Dr. Snuggles gets off the phone after an hour of guy talk with a friend or one of our sons.

I've gone through seasons when I felt very alone. After a move to another state, or leaving a church, we can feel like we're floating in a one-girl boat in the midst of a vast ocean. Leaving the office to work at home or retire can feel freeing, but you may still grieve the camaraderie you once knew. How do you start over?

Years ago, when I was just beginning to understand God's tug on my heart, I cried out to God for a Christian friend. Not long after, my best friend committed her life to Jesus. I joined a neighborhood Bible study. We got more involved in church. Today, when I thank God for the affirming, prayer-warrior sisters in my life, it's hard to believe there was a time when I didn't even have one.

God led me to a circle of Jesus-following women. If you don't have that kind of support yet, it's my prayer that He'll do the same for you. Joining a women's group or walking into a church when you don't know anyone can be scary, but it can also result in almost instant friends. As you share your joys and struggles, you'll likely feel a deeper bond with one or two women who just seem to get you. Treasure them. They're lifelines of mutual joy that can strengthen your marriage as well.

If you want to collect something, collect friends who make you a better person, a better friend, a better spouse.

— Cynthia —

Marriage is one of life's most important relationships. Getting married is the easy part (as many of us have found out by now). Staying married takes work. Staying *mutually satisfyingly* married (how many adverbs can one author use?) takes mega work, but it yields mega rewards.

You're waiting for a list, aren't you? All the mega rewards. See chapter 24 for more on that. What? The book only has twenty chapters? Huh. Well, it's in print now, so . . .

Before we were married, we knew the list well. Maybe even recited it in our sleep when we were single and longing. What we wanted in a spouse was this:

- Companionship
- Someone to share life
- A listening ear
- Another perspective in decision-making
- Intimacy (both body and soul)
- Belonging
- A fellow sojourner on life's journey, splitting the load, easing the load, understanding the load, shouldering the heavier part of the load . . .

In a particularly trying season of parenting adults, my husband and I stepped into one of those experiences of finding unexpected grace and strength to face what came next, and next, and next. On a day when the needle on my emotional gas tank was bouncing on *E* for empty, my husband sent me an email from work that said simply, "I'm here. Lean on me."

> **The truth is that no human being, not even a spouse, is capable of maintaining another person's happiness.**

It didn't occur to me until just now that comfort for my "*E* for empty" came through an "*E* for email." Lord, I noticed. Finally. Thanks for the sweet reminder that You are more creative than all of us combined.

Often, my husband is that "lean on me" friend. But the truth is that no human being, not even a spouse, is capable of maintaining another person's happiness.

So sometimes my comfort comes through one of my sisters or sisters-in-law. Or my daughter. Or daughter-in-law. Or a forever friend like Becky or Sheryl or Kristin. Or a trusted friend from church.

If all my leaning moments were relegated to the spouse in my house, a spouse who sometimes is as heavyhearted as I am about whatever drained me—and frankly, sometimes it's the *spouse* who drains me—he'd soon collapse under the weight. His tolerance for brainstorming is different than mine. His own unspoken concerns already take up plenty of room on his shoulders.

Ultimately, yes, Jesus is the strongest and most reliable leaning post. But it was God's design that we help shoulder each other's burdens. The friends who share a common interest that is of no interest to my husband, or who can identify with my complaints about still trying to lose that baby weight (the child is now thirty-four), or who have listening capacity left over when I've completely worn out my husband's supply play a vital role in keeping my marriage strong.

Did that sound odd to your ears or heart? That having someone *other* than my husband as a friend makes me a better friend for my husband? If the temperament of your marriage or your individual personalities is improved by the relationship he has with his friends and you have with yours, if time with friends relieves the feeling of too-much-of-a-good-thing togetherness, why would we fight or feel guilty about that?

When we're stuck in rough circumstances, the *friendship* part of our relationships can't help but make the challenges easier to bear. And that works both in the friendship factor with our spouse and when we allow each other friends who meet the verbiage or interest needs we can't fulfill.

Consider Ecclesiastes 4:9–10: "Two are better than one, because they have a good return for their labor: If either of them falls down, one can help the other up. But pity anyone who falls and has no one to help them up."

Some use these verses to support what they consider the misery of singleness. But in its original language, this passage wasn't speaking to husbands and wives, as we might assume, although it certainly applies. This Scripture is speaking about coworkers and friends.

The Hebrew word for "the other" is *chaber*, meaning a companion, fellow, "knit together," or an associate (according to *Strong's Exhaustive Concordance*[4]). Friend. Co-laborer. A husband and wife who are knit together? Husband and wife companions helping each other succeed, assisting when we fall or need a place to lean? Sure.

But it's intriguing that the Bible didn't specify the marriage relationship here, although marriage was an applauded status for those reading the words when they were first written. Rather, this passage encompasses friends assisting when we need to be uplifted, helped to our feet again.

If I return from a girls' night out resentful of my spouse, irritated, short-tempered, or too tired to be civil, either the mix of friends was unhealthy or my focus was misplaced. But if I come home refreshed, more patient, encouraged, and breathing more freely, haven't the outside friendships served as a relief valve for both my husband and me?

Social connections are an important component of mental health, we're often told. Developing deep or emotionally stronger friendships seems to come more easily to women than men. With fewer close relationships, some men lean on their wives to maintain social connections for both of them. They *depend* on their wives, socially. In some cases, that can lead to a husband expecting to be the sole object of his wife's attention, especially in retirement. It's not hard to imagine how unrealistic and unhealthy that can be for both of them.

From college days, Wonderhubby has craved time in the wilds of Canada, northern Minnesota, or the Upper Peninsula of Michigan. The more remote, the better, to his way of thinking. Even years when we couldn't swing a family vacation, he would find a way (and a buddy) so he could dip his canoe paddle in wilderness waters.

I accompanied him on several trips, but it soon became evident that listening to the relaxing sounds of bears and wolves circling the tent was more his thing than mine. It took awhile, but I got over the misconception that he was "leaving me" to head for the wilderness with one or more of his friends. He came home with weeks' worth of stories to tell, and with his soul glowing almost as brightly as his deeply tanned arms.

He needed that time with the guys. Still does.

If I held on to resentment over his going off and having fun, neither of us would have been happy. Respecting his need for guy friends and guy activities strengthened our marriage. And his tolerance is high when I tell him I need to escape with our daughter for our almost-annual five-day getaway to a location with lots of nature, woodland trails, sky and sun and water and flowers, flush toilets, fancy restaurants, and cute little gift shops.

We do our spouse a disservice if we expect them to be the only person we will lean on, or if we have nothing more to contribute to our conversations because we're together 24/7, both seeing the same sights and hearing the same sounds.

(And no, that wasn't a reference to wilderness camp man-noises.)

CHAPTER 15

I Need a New Nameplate

— Becky —

I have two friends who had to give up teaching careers they loved because of health problems. One had a hubby working from home; the other's SITH was retired. Both men were happy in what they did to fill their days, but my friends were lost. "Teacher" wasn't just a job description; it was a "me" description.

Can you relate?

You used to know who you were. You had a title and a job description. Full-time mom. Educator. Business manager. Executive assistant. Executive. Salesperson. Marketing director. Doctor. Maybe the title is still yours, but you work from home. There's no nameplate on the door. There's no door at all.

"Who am I now?" you ask. The affirmations are gone, and so are the respect and camaraderie of coworkers or, for parents whose nests have emptied, the companionship of children. It's likely your SITH is dealing with a similar loss of identity too.

There are choices at this *Y* in the path, but none of them are clear-cut. The sign on the left reads Self-Pity Street, while the one on the right says Reinvent Yourself Road. Both can lure you, but both can be scary. In truth, most of us blaze a winding path between the two for a while.

One day, you huddle under a blanket, flipping through old photos, texts, and emails on your phone, remembering who you once were. Under that blankie, our old lives can shine brighter than they ever did in real time. The next day may find you with sharpened pencils and a never-touched yellow legal pad, or tingling fingers hovering over computer keys as you stare at the inviting emptiness of a new document. At the top of the page? *Goals!*

Before we even take a step onto the nostalgia-paved left road, we know it's only going to feel good for the first few miles. On a feeling-sorry-for-ourselves journey, the pavement ends suddenly, and gravel starts to hurt our feet. The shiny possibilities of the other path beckon. We love fresh starts . . . until we look around and don't know where we are. Nothing looks familiar. Confusion multiplies if that person we promised to accompany no matter where life leads is way out ahead, crushing this "new me" thing. Or far behind under his own blankie.

How do we negotiate sharp, unseen turns and enjoy the beauty of unexpected vistas if our person has a GPS set for different coordinates than ours?

I remember more than one family vacation when my dad thrust a cockeyed-folded map across the front seat at my mom and impatiently told (not asked) her to figure out where he was supposed to turn next. I hated sitting in the back seat helplessly watching my mom fight tears as she fumbled with a paper as wide as she was tall.

Life is hard when we're not in sync. As writers, Cynthia and I have no intention of retiring until an editor or agent clears her throat and sweetly says, "I'm afraid you've lost it, dear. Your muse has muted itself." Our husbands happen to have different philosophies about this stage of life. They aren't opposed to work, as long as they get to decide when and how. And as long as it doesn't cut into hard-earned R & R.

In the book of Psalms, we read, "The LORD makes firm the

steps of the one who delights in him" (37:23), and "Your word is a lamp for my feet, a light on my path" (119:105). Clearly, when we seek God's guidance, He directs our paths. But what if my spouse's path is all downhill and mine is a steep climb? Can we still be on the same journey?

> At the time we retired we were both working about fifty hours a week and at meetings at least two nights a week. We knew there would be potential for challenges to our relationship if we were together 24/7. It's important to redirect your energy and gifts to volunteer work. [My wife] has kept her nurse's license current so she is able to work at free clinics in the States and at mission sites abroad. I have tried to use my experience in education in a similar way. We have found that it is important not to abandon your career but to redefine it.
>
> —Dan A.

As I've mentioned before, the first few weeks of 24/7 togetherness were rough for me. Mostly because "Mine!" was still so much a part of my vocabulary. My house. My time. My schedule. My way.

I knew who I was in Me World. Part-time writer. Part-time wife. Those two halves fit nicely together. Not that I ever actually took time off from wife-ing, but all the wifely things I had been doing to nurture our marriage during the thirty-five hours he was chiropractoring—planning meals, laundry, cleaning, praying for him—could be perfectly synced to the rhythm of my daily word-count goals. Finish a scene; switch the laundry. Hit a thousand words; start supper. I was afraid full-time wife-ing would eclipse everything else. My creative side would get lost in the shadow of those giant letters: W-I-F-E. I was in full-on HHATT mode.

My fears were not only unfounded, they were also dumb. I'm still me . . . just more a part of a *we* than I was before. I also realized, later than I should have, that my man had his own Me World that was actually changing more drastically than mine. No more sign out front telling the whole world he had letters behind his name. No more staff depending on him. No more drafting care plans that helped people get back to work, avoid surgery, resume normal life. No more patients telling him he was amazing, wonderful, the answer to their prayers.

When I finally poked my head out of my Me World, I saw him at the *Y* in the road, looking a bit bewildered. Thankfully, he didn't thrust a wrinkled map at me and ask me to tell him which way to turn. We started a dialogue full of "We could do . . ." and "I think I'd like to try . . ." He took my hand and we angled off to the right together. "This is going to be an adventure," I said.

The talents and passions God has given you don't need to get packed in a cardboard box along with that old nameplate. Ask Him to show you how to use those gifts and passions in a new way.

Sure, there are potholes along the way, even when you're a member of the We're Home All the Time Club. Yep, we both have days of wandering back to Self-Pity Street, but we're helping each other figure out who we want to be on Reinvent Yourself Road.

I watched my teacher friends travel this road. Funny thing is, they're still teaching. Not in a classroom, but on mission trips, in Bible studies, and with homeschooling grandchildren. The talents and passions God has given you don't need to get packed in a cardboard box along with that old nameplate. Ask Him to show you how to use those gifts and passions in a new way.

Some mornings, when Dr. Snuggles heads out for a five-mile run and I join him on my bike, we leave the driveway at the same time. But when we get to the top of the hill, I *schwoop* down, leaving him far behind. I'll ride ahead, then circle back to meet him. We'll chat for a bit, then I'll move on at a faster pace than he's keeping. I might take off and do an extra couple of miles, then end up back at our driveway just as he reaches it. He's a runner. I'm a bicycle rider. Yet we're on the same road, going to the same place. A lot like life.

We read in Genesis, "Therefore a man shall leave his father and his mother and hold fast to his wife, and they shall become one flesh" (2:24 ESV). We often think of this as becoming one physically and forget that our brains are also involved in this union. That's where we run into snags, isn't it? There's nothing easy about joining the thoughts, feelings, goals, dreams, aspirations, and expectations of two distinct individuals into one mutually satisfying whole without losing our precious, God-given uniqueness.

Since "one flesh" was God's idea, I love knowing I can trust His written Word for instructions.

The apostle Paul implores his readers in his letter to the Ephesians "to live a life worthy of the calling you have received. Be completely humble and gentle; be patient, bearing with one another in love. Make every effort to keep the unity of the Spirit through the bond of peace" (4:1–3).

Humility. Gentleness. Patience. Diligence in keeping peace. Even if my spouse's path is all downhill and mine is a steep climb, striving for these things daily, with the Lord's help, can keep us on the same ever-after journey. It may not be an easy trek, but isn't a measure of marital "unity of the Spirit through the bond of peace" worth the effort?

— Cynthia —

Home Sweet Office.

Home Sweet Research and Development Department.

Home Sweet Hospice Unit.

Home Sweet Rehab Center.

Home Sweet Battlefield.

Those signs may hang invisibly over the front door or on the walls of our houses during the course of a lifetime together. And—except for the battlefield example—they may all indicate a necessary function of our home. But we can't afford to have any of these functions become the definition of the house we share.

As individuals, we struggle to figure out new roles when we're called to them or they're thrust upon us. Caregiver, spouse's occupational therapist, spouse's executive assistant, the retired one, coworker, advocate . . .

Roles, not identities.

> **Sometimes home needs to become a temporary or long-term classroom. Home is a place to recuperate. Home is the base of operations for a business. But it can't lose its identity as *home*.**

Sometimes home needs to become a temporary or long-term classroom. Home is a place to recuperate. Home is the base of operations for a business. But it can't lose its identity as *home*. It's meant to be Home Sweet Haven.

As mentioned earlier, I've worked from home for all but a few years of our marriage. Working from home is deeper than the idea of working from *house*. Home is a dwelling place, sanctuary, safe harbor, and refuge, the "place" that goes with you when you move to a new apartment or house.

Home doesn't need a new nameplate, even if *we* do through the seasons and upheavals of life. Home is still—or needs to be—a place where we belong.

Belong.

What habits can we adjust so we're communicating to ourselves, our spouse, our children and grandchildren, and our neighbors that home—our home—is a safe haven, whether they're in it for an hour, a week, eighteen years, or forever?

A soldier stands at the door, shouldering a rucksack, hat in hand. His or her family opens the door wide and says, "Welcome home."

The scene clutches at our hearts, no matter how many times we've witnessed it in movies, television, or real life. So much is encapsulated in the wonder of the words "Welcome home."

Would you agree that too often when our spouse comes through the door, our first words—if we even acknowledge our loved one's arrival—are more likely these?

"Hey."

"Did you remember to get milk?"

"You will not believe what the washing machine is doing."

"Brace yourself. We have to talk."

"Oh, home so soon?"

"What took you so long?"

What if we honored the concept of home as a place to belong no matter what's going on in life, no matter how much time we spend in that space together, no matter how heavy the concerns of our hearts, no matter what each of our new nameplates indicate? What if we considered our new, compelling role that of making home a haven? What if we started every reentry moment with an atmosphere of, if not the actual words, "Welcome home"?

In times of excess togetherness, do you consider yourself "stuck" at home or "safe" at home with your spouse? How do you protect against the first and guard the second? For me, my nemesis and friend Attitude makes all the difference.

If Attitude crawls out of bed in the morning with her looking-for-flaws, life's-not-fair, somehow-every-hard-thing-must-be-his-fault voice gnatting it up in my ear, she'll find plenty of support for her point of view, and influence me whether I want to listen to her or not.

If, on the other hand, Attitude wakes up with her look-for-the-good, life's-hard-but-glorious, somehow-every-difficult-thing-will-work-out-if-we-work-together song filling the air, the atmosphere changes. My spouse's presence in the house is not an intrusion or interruption or irritation, but a fresh day's opportunity to demonstrate the way God loves me through the way I love the human closest to me.

I don't know about you, but I had to read that last sentence again.

God's overarching message is this: "You're safe here with Me." A God-honoring marriage communicates the same. "You're safe here with me. Your flaws, your quirks, your idiosyncrasies, your fears, your heart's desires, your uncertainties, your needs—expressed or unexpressed—are all safe here with me."

If you're reading this and home is not a safe place where you *know* every day—even on the imperfect ones—that you belong, your new nameplate is going to have a hard time staying upright. *You* will have a hard time staying upright, without help.

If you feel that the walls are closing in, that's normal. If you feel you're sometimes unappreciated, also normal. If you feel drained, that's normal.

If you feel in danger, that's not normal. See the end of the book for resources to help you know where to turn for help sorting through what's fixable and what isn't. It may all *feel* unfixable to you, but don't lean on that as your final answer until you've reached out for help from a trusted professional.

Back to the home's nameplate:

Home Sweet Shelter from the Storm.

Home Sweet Soul Spa.

Home Sweet Just-the-Right-Amount-of-Togetherness.

Becky: "I thought this was a chapter about figuring out who and what we are in this new stage of life?"

Cynthia: "It is. Home is who we are."

Becky: "Ah!"

Cynthia: "Yep. No matter what else we do, or what roles we hold, this remains the same—we are preservers and caretakers of all the beautiful descriptors of a place our spouse's heart can call home."

CHAPTER 16

Familiarity Breeds Meh

— Becky —

Ever have one of those mornings when you roll over in bed and stare at that peacefully sleeping hunk of man and you just can't help but . . . yawn?

Asking for a friend.

Remember when you thought being together 24/7 was going to be just like your dating days, only better? All this time together to hold hands, snuggle, talk about feelings, gaze into each other's eyes, sneak off for some afternoon delight whenever and wherever . . .

Okay, so maybe your illusions weren't quite that unrealistic. But maybe you harbored a weak hope that the opposite of "out of sight, out of mind" would kick in once you were in each other's line of sight all day.

So what happened?

He works in one room, you work in the other, in your slouchy, comfy clothes. You sit in your separate recliners watching TV while you eat supper. You wake up at different times, go to bed at different times. The sizzle has fizzled.

Boredom can cause an otherwise stable marriage to stall out and take a nosedive into choppy seas. What do you do when you've stopped climbing and the engine is about to seize up?

I wish I could say I was writing this from a calm yet exhilarating marriage-cruising altitude, doling out the wisdom I learned on the way to bliss. In truth, I've had moments of texting Cynthia with cryptic messages like, "Why, again, did we think we were qualified to write this?" or "Shouldn't I be in a better place by now? Who wants to take advice from someone who yawns when she—" Oh, wait, sorry. That was a friend of mine.

Just know that the only thing we're experts at is the been-here-before-rewind-start-over cycle. But there have been victories along the way. We've learned a few things about marriage nosedives we're happy to share.

1. *Wait it out.* I'm starting with the simplest suggestion here. It's the one I've often given when asked to share some pithy advice at a bridal shower. I hate hinting to a head-in-the-clouds bride-to-be that the day is coming when she'll wake up and yawn at the man she now believes hung the stars, but a little advance warning can keep a molehill a molehill.

In the absence of any definable problem, a sense of apathy about your knight in shining armor may be caused by a bad dream about him, reading a too-good-to-be-true romance novel, listening to your best friend share something amazing her man did (the comparison monster is ugly!), or eating too much taco dip before bed. Or him eating too much taco dip before bed. If you can't put your finger on an actual problem, give it forty-eight hours. Two days from now your knight may suddenly be back on his white charger.

2. *Look back.* A little nostalgia can be as invigorating as an energy drink. Get out the old pictures and love letters, curl up in a comfy chair, and step back in time. Invite your man to join you on a "remember when" date. Talking about that first date, first kiss, your favorite places to walk, and those long phone conversations can rekindle some of the feelings that got lost in the shuffle of work and kids. A word of caution, though. Avoid the land mines

of comparing then and now: "Remember when you had hair?" "Remember when you still fit into that dress?" "Remember when you used to pay attention to me?" "Remember when you laughed at my jokes?"

The smartest thing my wife and I did was divide up our days into projects that we did together and separately. This allowed us to maintain a habit of working and then sharing stories of both our progress and delays without "fixing" each other or coaching.

The wisest thing we did was watch carefully for a window of time to leave home and go away together to the beach for five days. We decided to make this a secret and planned it like a mission. No social media or anything to alert our circle that we were up to something. It came together and we enjoyed the change of scenery and outdoor time. It really helped us to break the routine around our home and adjust our expectations for the new "normal" as we returned home.

—Steve Methvin, husband for thirty-eight years, with three married children and three grandchildren

3. *Plan something fun.* The Couples Institute has a great list of seventy-five creative ways to add some pizzazz to what can easily become ho-hum days.[1] We tried a few of their suggestions, added some of our own, and now have several still in regular rotation. Here are a few of our favorites:

- *Bake or cook together.* Our lunches have become shoulder-to-shoulder scavenge-the-fridge-for-leftovers times. Nudging each other away from the silverware drawer or seeing who can get their plate in the microwave first turns a mundane, necessary task of life into an opportunity for playfulness.
- *Draw.* You don't have to be artistic to do this. In fact, it

may even be more fun if you aren't because it brings more humor into it. Maybe even draw portraits of each other. Dr. Snuggles is discovering some long-dormant talent. I, on the other hand, can't compete with our six-year-old grandchildren. But it's still fun.

- *Dance.* Slow and romantic or fast and silly. Either way will gift you with a sense of connection. Kids around? Let them join in!

- *Exercise.* I'd told Dr. Snuggles that yoga stretches would help his running, but it took months of nagging to finally get him on the floor attempting a pigeon pose. The result was laughter and a vow to never try yoga again. But anything that results in mutual laughter counts as success.

- *Listen to an audiobook or podcast.* Our church did an eight-session YouTube series called "Tough Topics." We watched it together and then spent time talking about subjects that didn't normally come up in conversation.

> [My husband and I] have become masters of the "text flirt." We might be both working from home, in sight of each other many times a day, eating meals together, but underneath the daily, sometime mundane tasks, we have created an affair of the heart—*with each other!* By fanning the flame of romance and intimacy as the undercurrent of our marriage, our relationship feels young and exciting.
>
> —Pam Farrel, author of *52 Ways to Wow Your Husband*

- *Plan a future trip.* "Where do you want to go for vacation?" is a question that can spark fun dreaming together. Even if, realistically, you know you only have the time and budget for a long camping weekend, it's still fun to plan that "someday, if only" vacay. Pretend you're independently wealthy. Close your eyes and imagine the two of you sipping umbrella drinks in your private infinity pool next to your all-inclusive overwater bungalow on stilts on Mexico's Maroma Beach. Then go make tacos together!

- *Break out the board games.* For years after our kids left home, board games only came out when grandkids were over. But we've revived the fun as part of our new retirement routines. We have some fierce but friendly competition over Ticket to Ride, Port Royal, and Splendor.

- *Use clean socks, roll them up individually, and have a "snowball" fight.* I had to laugh at this one from the Couples Institute. I've done this with our youngest son's five boys. We built barricades out of couch cushions and let the socks fly. Never thought of doing this with Dr. Snuggles, but there's always a first time. Duck, honey!

> **A little creative thinking can give you a list of go-to things to do together that can banish yawns and reignite fading embers.**

A little creative thinking can give you a list of go-to things to do together that can banish yawns and reignite fading embers.

— Cynthia —

What if we could turn misunderstanding into understanding, aggravation into adaptation, and dying embers of love into glorious, unquenchable flames? Yes, even during a season of what seems like too much togetherness.

God is all for that idea. In Romans 15:5 we read that God, who gives patience, steadiness, and encouragement, wants us to live in complete harmony with one another—each with the attitude of Christ toward the other.

When looking for expertly tight harmonies, a music teacher or choir director will often ask for two experiments. Rather than looking at their music, vocalists are encouraged to look at each other. Granted, except for serious-minded students, at the middle school level that can lead to the giggling equivalent of a food fight. But more mature musicians who try the experiment sound better. How did watching each other improve their harmony?

Intriguing, isn't it?

Then the same vocal instructor or choir director will ask the vocalists to close their eyes and sing through the same section of music. They quickly learn to listen for a breath, the slightest crescendo, and the precise tone with which they are harmonizing. Not something in the general vicinity of the pitch, but so closely aligned that without knowing it, they master the art of precision downbeats and end notes and even mimic each other's slight nuances in vibrato.

They listen so intently and adjust to each other so carefully, undistracted by other things, that the musicians discover cues about each another that lend to better harmony. Ultimately that leads to a more satisfying musical experience for both the musicians and the audience.

It's not hard to imagine how that could apply to times in our lives when we seem out of sync with the one we love, or less keenly aware of their "nuances." We feel like we're singing "Row, Row, Row Your Boat" on an endless loop. Where's the excitement in that?

Unison when done well is lovely. Harmony when done well can be soul-stirring.

And isn't that what we want? To fill our home with harmony, not discord? Or awkward silence?

We'll be far better off if we recognize early in the process that if we want to honor God with our lives, every step we take is an adjustment to others and a realignment to God's perspective and desires for us.

You won't find it surprising that an hour before putting these words to paper, Wonderhubby and I were standing in the kitchen having a discussion about something we may or may not have hashed into slimy little bits of meh a dozen-to-the-tenth-power times in our marriage. I don't know what was in his mind, but in mine, I saw myself in a place where I could:

- *Give in for the sake of peace but solve nothing.* In essence, letting the subject return to a state of meh—uninspiring, unexceptional, lacking interest or enthusiasm or resolution.
- *Keep pressing in, defending my position,* which I frankly thought could rival a high-priced lawyer's closing arguments in a tough case.
- *Find a way to bless him.*

As soon as I'd quieted my heart enough to hear the "bless him" option, I had my answer. Who would settle for *meh* if they could convert it to *bless*? Propelled by what I knew was the Holy Spirit rather than my nature, I said, "I wonder if what we both need to do right now is to cut each other some slack."

Who would settle for *meh* if they could convert it to *bless*?

He looked up, a visible sense of relief on his face. "Yeah."

I moved to his side of the kitchen island and wrapped my arms around his shoulders. "What if we cut each other big swaths of slack so we can get through this?"

(In this case, "this" was the remodeling project that had deteriorated from an adventure into how-long-is-this-thing-gonna-last-and-will-we-survive-one-more-difference-of-opinion-about-what-constitutes-straight-and-level?)

The bless-him route had a great return on investment. Peace reigned once again. Productivity increased. And we were high-fiving each other for figuring out a tough calculation for minimizing the wonkiness of the walls of this old, old house.

Meh can sometimes simply mean "Yeah, whatever." Or "Don't care . . . and I don't mean that in the I-really-have-no-opinion-on-this-issue way." And sometimes meh is a state of being, when togetherness to the max over time leads us to define success as tolerating each other pretty well. Like a coworker you are stuck with and find ways to work around but would never invite to lunch.

Nothing in God's way of doing life opts for "Yeah, whatever." He is a relational God. His is a plan for excellence, for ongoing growth, for abundance. He is a passionate God who applauds wholehearted devotion (Psalm 119:10) and an all-in mentality. If He is pained when His people's love for Him turns lukewarm (Revelation 3:16)—becomes meh—why wouldn't He feel the same way about a union He instituted and blesses?

God's Meh Antidote

O Lord, God of Israel, there is no God like you in all of heaven above or on the earth below. You keep your covenant and show unfailing love to all who walk before you in *wholehearted* devotion. (1 Kings 8:23 NLT, emphasis added)

And whatever you do, in word or deed, do everything in the name of the Lord Jesus, giving thanks to God the Father through him. (Colossians 3:17 ESV)

Whatever you do, work heartily, as for the Lord and not for men, knowing that from the Lord you will receive the inheritance as your reward. You are serving the Lord Christ. (Colossians 3:23–24 ESV)

And this is my prayer: that your love may abound more and more in knowledge and depth of insight, so that you may be able to discern what is best and may be pure and blameless for the day of Christ. (Philippians 1:9–10)

Finally, brothers and sisters, whatever is true, whatever is noble, whatever is right, whatever is pure, whatever is lovely, whatever is admirable—if anything is excellent or praiseworthy—think about such things. (Philippians 4:8)

Authors and speakers Bill and Pam Farrel (how many Bills can we work into this book? Becky's Bill, Cynthia's Bill, Pam's Bill, the grocery bill—oh, wait, different chapter) often say that the question is not "How can we be like *that* couple?" or "How can we do this right?" but "How can we be the best us?"

Sailors are well familiar with the doldrums, which is far more than a concept. *Doldrums* is a nautical term referring to the invisible band around the earth near the equator where trade winds blow steadily on either side but are absent within the band. Sailing ships sometimes get mired on windless waters in the doldrums. They want to move forward but are kept from it. The listlessness of a seemingly endless stream of doldrum days has been known to drive even veteran sailors mad. They can't reach their destination. Can't turn back. They drift so slowly they're hardly moving and remain in a suffocating stillness.

Who wants to admit that our marriages can drift into a pattern of windless days? No forward current. Nothing to fill our souls' sails. We're still in the sailboat. Still together. But not only are we immobile, we're draining our rations and eyeing each other as if our partner is the reason the wind isn't blowing.

Especially during stressful times, or either voluntary or involuntary confinement in the same space, or in the days or seasons when our marriage's sails have no wind in them, survival depends on our attitude toward one another, on implementing creative measures for endurance, and on our commitment to wait it out.

The only people who don't come out of the doldrums are those who self-sabotage, give up too soon, or eat each other.

Harsh? If our words bite, our attitude butchers, or we begin to view our mate as the adversary in the doldrums, we metaphorically cannibalize our marriage. An empty sailboat will eventually drift to shore.

Doldrums are a naturally occurring phenomenon. In a marriage, they sometimes hit because a husband and wife have neglected to pay attention to the telltale signs that they were drifting that direction. Is it time to send out a distress signal first to God, who brought you together, then if necessary to a trained counselor?

CHAPTER 17

Circadian Algorithms: Solving the Problem of Differing Schedule Preferences

— Cynthia —

Friends of ours live in a tiny floating house. To be more accurate, they (two couples, actually) live on sailboats. Their 24/7 spouse-in-the-galley-salon-or-poop-deck lifestyle could make me feel guilty for complaining about the eighteen-inch walkway my husband and I navigated dozens of times a day until, forty-two years later, we were able to breathe the glorious air of open concept living. But our friends' experiences have fed me ideas for coping with awkward rhythms, circadian and otherwise.

One sailboat-living wife—Pam Farrel, author of the bestselling *Men Are Like Waffles, Women Are Like Spaghetti*—says, "If I sing and pray aloud, it can disturb [my husband]. The space is that small. We share a ministry but also have individual ministries and businesses, so we have to stagger our phone calls and especially video meetings because we both talk louder and louder when we get excited about a project we're working on. So even if we choose opposite ends of the vessel, we can never both be on a phone call or video call at the same time."

Maybe in your marriage it's different bedtimes. Different ideas about how much time is "enough" time with the grandchildren.

Different needs for socializing, quiet, being on the road (or the water) and being home. Those circadian and personality algorithms can throw off our rhythm as a couple if we aren't conscious of them, respectful of the differences, and intentional about stepping back to let the other take the lead once in a while.

We don't decide lifetime marriage commitments by comparing our answers on an "Are We the Same Person?" application. In what marriage do *both* partners find five thirty the ideal time to rise, shifted to compensate for the vernal equinox? In what marriage do both find a second wind at nine and work in a spurt until midnight? (Those people are not getting adequate sleep if they rise at dawn and go to bed at midnight, by the way.)

Now, it is possible that both parties think cilantro tastes like soap, despite genetic discoveries that say a soapy aftertaste is only an issue for 4 to 14 percent of humans. Sure sign of marriage compatibility, right?

If we search for a mate whose internal rhythms and every interest are identical to ours, we're marrying ourselves. And that kind of defeats the purpose.

If we search for a mate whose internal rhythms and every interest are identical to ours, we're marrying ourselves. And that kind of defeats the purpose. It also sets us up for a narrow life, for stories with only one point of view, and for a lack of stimulating conversations (sometimes known as intense discussions).

A friend of mine says she and her husband seem to be off by two hours, as if they live in two different time zones in the same house. He likes to get up two hours before she's ready for the day, and she has two hours of energy left when he's ready to call it a night.

Other friends have told me their own challenges and coping mechanisms for differing schedule preferences.

Casey said, "My husband is usually gone before the rest of us wake up in the morning and falls asleep way before I do. With him home half of the week now, it's a bit of an adjustment. He was standing at the edge of the bed one morning as if to say, 'Okay, it's time to start moving.'"

Kelly said, "My husband and I are relearning how to adjust to different sleep patterns after being on opposite shifts for seven years. My husband worked overnights, but he lost his job recently. Now he is home all the time, including at night. I finally told him I have kept vigilant watch over our house and kids for seven years, so every time he gets up in the middle of the night, it wakes me. He might think he needs that 3 a.m. snack, but I need my sleep!"

My friend Billie said, "He knows I'm a better human if I sleep!"

Michelle said, "Regarding differing bedtime rhythms? We met in the middle!"

One common thread among my friends who responded to the question about wake-sleep conflicts was courtesy. There's that word again. Couples who thrive despite their circadian differences show each other the courtesy of being "devoted to one another in love. Honor one another above yourselves" (Romans 12:10). In other words, we're to be devoted to each other and work to excel at showing respect for each other.

If I mock my spouse's wake-sleep preferences or natural cycle, I'm constructing a wall in our relationship. If I give in to his preferences, I may lose my best REM sleep.

That happened to me. Lingering lethargy turned out to be a sleep disorder exacerbated by my getting up early to fix my husband his breakfast and pack a lunch for his workday. A medical study showed I was consistently missing my body's natural rhythm of REM sleep, the most restorative and deepest portions of the sleep cycle. My doctor prescribed that I find other ways to bless my husband so I didn't perpetuate the REM sleep deprivation.

Not one to disobey a doctor's orders, I talked to Wonder-hubby about the prescribed plan. He agreed that my health required that I sleep later in the morning, and he began making his own lunch and breakfast on workdays. He missed my making him breakfast on those days, although he grew quite fond of microwave breakfast sandwiches. We both missed starting our day together on his working days. But many things improved for us as a couple and for me personally when sleep deprivation waned.

Now that we're members of the WHATT Club, we start almost every day together and share a sweet time of devotions. I'm back to making breakfast . . . after enjoying a healthy dose of REM sleep.

He honors my needs. I, in turn, don't play music past his bedtime unless I'm listening through headphones or earbuds. If there's a television show we both enjoy but it comes on after he's already climbing the stairs to the siren call of his pillow, I record it so we can watch it together.

Even though it's just the two of us in the house now, I cook big batches of whatever we're having for supper so there's always something tasty in the fridge to reheat if his circadian rhythm tells him he's hungry for lunch long before I am.

It's not a contest, but it is a heartwarming practice to focus on outdoing each other in thoughtfulness.

--- Becky ---

Julie got out of bed at seven and wandered from room to room in a quiet house before realizing her husband wasn't there. Again.

No note on the kitchen counter. No text. Had Jesus returned to claim His church and she'd been left behind? Nope. Just another episode in The Disappearance of George.

George is a morning person. A get-up-at-four-and-be-on-the-lake-by-five person. And he wants his wife by his side. Julie doesn't mind fishing . . . after the sun is high enough in the sky that she can see to bait the hook without turning into bait herself.

After thirty years of being behind her desk by eight o'clock, five days a week, in a high-powered office, the last thing she wants to do is jump out of bed before the sun, slurp coffee from a travel mug, and breakfast on a plain bagel. She loves leisurely stretching in bed, pointing her toes toward the empty span of mattress vacated hours before by her restless man. Coffee is a ritual of grinding beans, heating water, letting it steep in her French press, adding three dollops of hazelnut creamer, and blending it into a frothy confection . . . to be slowly sipped while reading her Bible and savoring a toasted bagel with cream cheese and strawberry jam in the sunroom.

Julie has reason to wonder why God matched her with a person who doesn't match her at all.

Can you relate? I was raised by a morning person. Until I reached these "autumn years," I would have preferred not to see the sun until it had ascended halfway to lunchtime. My mother got some kind of perverse pleasure out of cranking up the music on the living room stereo and skipping into my room, cheerily announcing, "Muffins and fresh Tang! Rise and shine!" while yanking open the curtains so spikes of sunlight could stab my happily snoozing eyes. (You're right, I really should see a counselor about my not-so-repressed anger.)

Thankfully, I married a man who, though he gets out of bed before me on most days, starts his day quietly . . . and doesn't long for me to bait hooks at five in the morning. But our differences do cause some issues.

From the time we were newlyweds, we've gone to bed at the same time most nights. We both read for a while, and then he puts down his iPad and kisses me, and I keep reading . . . sometimes for an hour or more. If my eyes are tired but my brain is still firing, I put in earbuds and listen to an audiobook or podcast or watch a movie. I usually feel drowsy around midnight.

Come morning, he's out of bed by six thirty, and I'll open my eyes an hour later, then catch up on news and social media on my phone for half an hour or more before easing out of bed.

Why not stay up until midnight if I'm not tired? That's a good question. I guess I've always looked at turning in at the same time as a bonding thing. Turning off the lights and locking the doors together brings closure to our day. Brushing our teeth together turns out not to be quite as romantic as I once imagined, and yet there is an element of intimacy in all we do at the end of the day. I take off my makeup—my public face—and we both slip into comfy pajamas. Not movie-worthy intimacy, but there's a comfortable vulnerability in these rituals no one else sees.

It's not just sleep schedules that can be out of sync. You may love being on the go from sunup to sundown, but he prefers taking things slow and scheduling time for naps. Our needs for socialization may be very different. If you're a bookworm married to a social butterfly, you'll both need a metamorphosis to make life work well.

If the bookworm sprouts wings to occasionally soar with her mate or the social butterfly chooses to flutter in place a little longer to spend time at ground level, they both experience something new.

Changing something about me in order for us to be more synchronized doesn't have to mean giving up who I am. If the bookworm sprouts wings to occasionally soar with her mate or the social butterfly chooses to flutter in place a little longer to spend time at ground level, they both experience something new.

Whether we're working from home or retired, 24/7 togetherness can often allow for far more flexibility—and grace—in our schedules. The grace part is important. Our friend Dave is one of those guys who loves to help his neighbors. Need someone to fix that leaky sink, till your garden, or run to the store for Grandma's meds? Dave is your guy. The phone rings, and he'll drop what he's doing to be there . . . even if it means dropping something off of his wife's priority list.

> What made home-all-the-time work for us is that I adjusted my work schedule so that I was available to help with the children and to create margin for her after managing five children all day. The best thing she did was to communicate exactly what she needed in that adjusted schedule.
>
> —Steven Montepeque, father of five

This caused a problem for decades when they were both working outside the home. He'd be halfway through weeding the garden on a Saturday afternoon when Joe down the street would call to ask for help tuning his engine. Shirley would come outside, garden gloves at the ready to work beside her man, and the tomato patch would be empty. Now that they're both retired, she's seeing Dave's big heart rather than just the big to-do list. Most of the time, anyway.

Dave and George could learn a thing or two about communication. Talking over the next day's plans every evening (while you're putting on those comfy jammies) can save a lot of frustration. If a neighbor calls, or the lake beckons, write or send a message. Shirley is learning to be more flexible about her lists too. Julie makes a sleep sacrifice every other Thursday morning, joining George on the boat, travel mug and cold bagel in hand as they watch the sunrise together.

It's the little things we do that add up to a life lived mostly in step with each other.

Navigating the Challenges of an Unexpected Season of "Home All the Time"

The smartest thing I did was to intentionally deepen my personal walk with God to cultivate a healthy attitude, and then build joyful diversions into the monotony of our days to engage our hearts—from games to home projects to special meal planning. The smartest thing my wife did was to use her gift of homemaking to keep our home cheerful, bright, smelling good, organized, and filled with good stuff. The wisest thing we did as a couple was to calmly, prayerfully, rationally, and personally talk through how we were feeling—especially when we found ourselves frustrated, combustible, or anxious.

—Cary Schmidt, pastor and author of *Stop Trying: How to Receive—Not Achieve—Your Real Identity*

CHAPTER 18

I Meant It When I Said "I Do" to the "In Sickness" Part of Our Vows

— Cynthia —

It's only three times my husband has almost died, right? One, two . . . Oh. Just two. Of which I am aware.

The first time, he was deep in the Canadian wilderness when a sudden illness hit with such force, it devastated his normally well-controlled diabetes. The doctors are still unsure if it was a raging gall bladder attack or pancreatitis. When he was finally rescued, he was on the verge of a diabetic coma from which he would likely not have rebounded. His personal physician estimated that if the rescue team had been even one hour later, they would have been recovering a lifeless body.

I was within an hour of becoming a too-young widow, a whisper-breath away from "until death do us part."

With no means of communication that far from civilization, he couldn't let me know he was in trouble, couldn't form a "Goodbye" that eventually wasn't needed. And he would have been gone before I had a chance to worry about him.

When I heard from the small, remote hospital that he was in intensive care, fighting his way back to life, twelve hours of a road trip separated us. Every single mile of that trip filled itself with questions. Was he truly out of the woods, in every sense of that phrase? Or was the damage to his system too much? The thoughts I didn't want to entertain came uninvited. Should I start thinking about funeral preparations, just in case? Even if he survived, would life as we knew it be the same or forever altered?

Three days later, they discharged him from the hospital into my care. I made a bed for him in the back of our van-turned-pretend-ambulance and was entrusted with the responsibility of keeping him alive for the twelve-hour trip home. While I drove. What were they thinking?

What was *I* thinking?

To what level will he recover? What's changed? Are we both going to be okay with that?

My feeling bad for him raced neck and neck with my feeling bad for me. I wasn't put out by inconveniences. My expectations had been upended—that he would always be the strong one physically, that he'd always be the one to provide and protect, that I could count on life proceeding according to plan.

> Although I'm so thankful to have the ability to work from home because of my husband's early-onset dementia, I miss my life. And as an introvert, I miss my privacy. As my husband becomes more childlike, he wants to be with me more and more. A shower without him bursting in to check on me seems like a rare treat these days. But whenever I feel this way, God reminds me that I won't always have him interrupting me or invading "my" space—and I set my selfishness aside as I turn back to him.
>
> —Marti Pieper, author and editor

From two lifetimes of upended expectations and sometimes devastating concerns, both Becky and I agree that the kind of love humans feel on our way to the altar isn't the same kind of love that can sustain a couple through all the highs and lows of marriage.

That proved true again thirteen years later when my husband fell from his hunting stand and broke his back and femur. The surgery to put the puzzle pieces of his femur back together kept him from using lower body strength to help him navigate post-accident life. And his broken back prevented him from using upper body strength. We were plunged back into an "I'm grateful you're alive, but man, this is hard" season of caregiving.

None of us can fully prepare for 24/7 together time that results from an accident, injury, or physical, emotional, or mental illness. Maybe you're the caregiver; maybe you're the one in need of care. Either way, you're feeling the strain on your marriage. This isn't the fun and carefree together time you dreamed of.

None of us pictured antidepressants and their side effects, bedpans and catheters, chemotherapy, panic attacks, daily migraines, or dementia when we made that "in sickness and in health" vow. You might feel trapped, helpless, or overworked, or that you're a burden.

"God has a plan" sounds cliché, but if we dissect the statement, we'll find practical solutions to make that vow resonate with the depth of meaning God had in mind when we stood at the altar.

God—the only one who has the power to change anything in our circumstances.

Has—present tense. We don't cry out to a God who then starts to work on a plan to rescue us. The Bible tells us he's already working his plan before the words leave our lips (see Isaiah 65:24).

> "God has a plan" sounds cliché, but if we dissect the statement, we'll find practical solutions to make that vow resonate with the depth of meaning God had in mind when we stood at the altar.

A plan—not wishful thinking. God doesn't operate from a position of hoping his idea will work but from a position of knowing what went before, what's happening now, and what the eventual outcome will be. We can't step into a situation—including illness- or diagnosis-forced togetherness—without his already having been there, setting the stage for us, and filling the shelves with what we will need.

You may have never entertained the idea of becoming a physical therapist, but you find yourself playing the role of one to help care for an injured or incapacitated spouse. You may have chosen the research lab over nursing as a career specifically so you'd never have to empty a bedpan, yet here you are. You may have found the very thing that most attracted you to your spouse—strength, physical fitness, sweet temperament—completely disappears in a time of "in sickness."

But you vowed . . .

Take heart. God is not unaware. He knows how different this may look from what you imagined. And a vow like a marriage commitment is witnessed—for legal purposes and vow-keeping reminders—by the other names on your marriage certificate, by your supportive family and friends, and by the God who knew about this eventuality before you said "I do."

If your spouse is ill, recuperating, or wracked by dementia or mental illness and you are your love's full-time caregiver, remember that the best thing you can do is to keep yourself physically, spiritually, emotionally, and mentally healthy. It's not selfish. It's part of your gift to the one you love.

— **Becky** —

Hannah meant every single promise she made to Alan before God and a church full of witnesses. Those shiny, wrapped-in-white-satin promises all seemed easily keepable. Until thirty years later when the man she'd vowed to love for better or for worse, in sickness and in health, began to change.

"Alan's depression has reframed my entire outlook for our retirement years," Hannah tells me. "He changed from a fun-loving, in-charge, and hard-working man into an insecure, fearful, dependent prisoner of his thoughts. Initially I was shell-shocked and in denial, wondering how I was going to get through this. I know *nothing* about this! I thought of my wedding vows now being challenged. Can our marriage survive? Will I stay?"

Can you imagine being in Hannah's shoes? Can you imagine it all too well?

Most marriages will face times when one spouse needs extra care and support and isn't able to keep up with normal responsibilities. Pregnancy, postpartum depression, short-term illness, surgery, injury. These seasons stretch our patience and may give our grace muscles a brutal workout. Thankfully, most of these seasons are temporary. We grow in these times. We find we are capable of more than we thought.

But what if it's not a season? What if it's a lifetime? Permanent disability, a lifestyle-altering chronic illness, a terminal diagnosis . . . Premarital counseling doesn't prepare anyone for these. We don't come into wedded bliss with a plan B for such crises.

This is dropped-in-the-deep-end, on-the-job training. And it can happen in week two of marriage, as it did for one of Cynthia's friends, or a week or more into retirement, or in the middle of a hurricane or layoff or sudden work-from-home order.

I'm not a fan of the buzz phrase "new normal," and yet it fits here. Just as a stroke victim must relearn walking and talking and other daily living activities, a couple whose world is turned upside down by unplanned togetherness must learn new skills. New ways of talking to each other, recognizing and expressing needs, serving, loving.

Hannah says, "Our communication skills have been hampered. I may withhold honesty in fear of making him feel worse. Our fun time together is greatly reduced. We've had to learn how to live on less money than previously and how to prioritize spending. I am no longer covered under my spouse's insurance and therefore that debt has increased. His depression has affected my physical health as well. I struggle with wanting my needs fulfilled and putting them aside to serve my spouse. I confess I also struggle with resentment, anger, and weariness. I've had to grieve the loss of what we had."

Grieving what you once had is normal, healthy, and needed. If you both have the ability and energy to talk through problems together or with a counselor, honesty can get you around a lot of roadblocks. Sometimes, though, talking isn't possible or may exacerbate feelings of inadequacy or the fear of being a burden.

If you both have the ability and energy to talk through problems together or with a counselor, honesty can get you around a lot of roadblocks.

I love Hannah's heart regarding her husband's depression: "This chaos drove me straight to the Lord. He promises to never leave me, and to give me strength and direction. It is by His grace alone I am here five years later. Softened, humbled, wiser, and more mature in my faith. I'm now open to God's plan and cast mine aside, trusting His Word: 'In their hearts humans plan their course, but the LORD establishes their steps'" (Proverbs 16:9).

Hannah says God is peeling back her layers of selfishness, disobedience, and pride. "The refining fire burns, yes. His love is the balm. It's for my good and, more importantly, His glory."

She adds, "I'm grateful for the rare good times with Alan, but I will often go hiking, to the movies, or to other places alone. My friends have been a circle of strength for me, praying and listening, though I won't openly share with those who know little about depression. It is a very hard disease to understand until you've lived it."

When I asked Hannah what advice she would give other women facing a similar trial, she was quick to answer. "Keep on keeping on and *pray, pray, pray*. Be humble and forgive often. As much as we think we can prepare for full-time togetherness, we cannot completely know the struggles until we're in them. That thought should cause us to lean into our Father. He will lead us."

It seems that every topic we've dealt with in this book brings us to one vital coping tool: grace. The word has several meanings. As a noun it can mean 1) "simple elegance or refinement of movement" or 2) "courteous goodwill." When used as a verb, as in "she graced him with her cheerful demeanor," it means "do honor or credit to (someone or something) by one's presence."[1]

We can use all these definitions when facing an "in sickness" challenge. "Simple elegance" as we stumble through learning new steps to unfamiliar music may seem unattainable. But the author of grace—the amazing kind—is a patient teacher and perfect gifter. The One who told the apostle Paul, "My grace is sufficient for you, for my power is made perfect in weakness" (2 Corinthians 12:9) knows what you are going through. When "courteous goodwill" seems beyond your abilities, ask Him for a little more—more patience, energy, joy, endurance, strength, love, kindness, mercy, grace—to get you through another day. As Hannah says, lean into Him. I pray God will allow you, and me, to "do honor" to our spouses by our very presence.

The "sickness" part of "in sickness and in health" is no less a vow than any other element of our commitment before God in marriage. Does that mean caring for an ill or aging or injured spouse comes naturally? Only to a few. The rest of us will find that season a time when pressing into the Lord is the daily infusion we need so His strength and His compassion flow through us.

—Cynthia

CHAPTER 19

Give Your SITH a Pass

— Becky —

Your husband is clueless.

No, I'm not jumping on the man-bashing bandwagon. Give me a minute to explain.

As I write this, I'm trying to get down from the high horse I've been perched on for a week. It all started last weekend when we had a houseful of family for three days. Before they arrived, I cleaned the house from top to bottom. I planned menus. I shopped. I cooked. I put sheets on beds and hung the good towels.

Dr. Snuggles mowed the lawn.

When our kids arrived, he went golfing with three of our sons. And sat. And ate. And slept. He did not cook or clear the table or wash the guest bathroom towels or interrupt his morning coffee to make breakfast for seven people or give up his daily run to lay out a buffet for twenty or empty wastebaskets or haul in the extra table and chairs from the garage.

Déjà vu from the early years of our marriage.

My resentment grew with each meal cooked and cleaned up by yours truly. Each passing hour found me adding to the litany of his wrongs scrolling through my head—and turning up the volume until this was all I could hear: *This may have been our system when he was gone thirty-plus hours a week and I was a stay-at-home mom, but the man is retired! He has time in spades. How could anyone be so rude? So thoughtless? So chauvinistic? He's turning into his dad. He thinks what I'm doing is women's work and he's too good for it. Too bad I'm too old to be barefoot and pregnant. What a good little woman I am, serving my man like he's all that and a bag of chips.*

It got ugly.

Doesn't self-righteousness feel amazing? Am I alone in reveling in martyrdom? In a previous chapter, I mentioned labeling my husband's way of doing things as different, not wrong. Not in this case. He was W-R-O-N-G.

I laid it all before the Lord, putting on a spread of my man's faults with the same joy I put into setting a pretty table with scrumptious food for our guests. Because, of course, God needed me to tell Him what was going on in my husband's small black heart.

By day four, the saddle on my high horse was starting to chafe a bit. Over the din in my head, I heard a quote from Oswald Chambers: "God never gives us discernment so that we may criticize, but that we may intercede."[1] But I *was* praying!

Hours after our kids left, we went to a parade in a nearby town and ran into a couple we know, though not well. Two minutes into catching up, the wife turned to me and thanked me for the marriage workshop I'd led six months earlier. "Your words helped me so much. So many great nuggets of wisdom. Especially 'don't expect your husband to be God.'"

Uh . . .

I smiled and thanked her, told her I was happy to hear it helped her. And cringed inside. *But* . . . wishing my husband would see how overburdened I was and pitch in with dishes wasn't expecting him to be God. Was it?

The talking point she was referring to focused on not expecting our husbands to read our minds. "Only God can do that," I told a roomful of women.

Well, sure, but . . . My whining grew louder. He should have known what I needed! It's just common courtesy. You don't need to be a mind reader to know the workload should be shared.

A tiny voice whispered, "You could have asked."

Grrr. Yes, I could have. And yes, he would have done anything I asked without complaining. "But that's not the point!" my pride answered.

The wrestling continued for days as I ignored all I knew and even *taught* about forgiveness and not letting the sun go down on your anger.

"Give him a pass." These words, spoken by a dear friend years earlier, began to seep into the pauses for breath between my rants. Cathy had shared how these four words were transforming her marriage. Whether her husband knowingly or cluelessly failed to meet her expectations, she was choosing to give him a free pass out of her resentment jail . . . freeing them both.

Finally, begrudgingly, I started the process myself. It wasn't an overnight fix. Though your experience may be different than mine, here are some give-him-a-pass steps that might help you too:

- *Pray. First. Always.* Ask God to help you see your husband's sins of omission or commission through God's eyes, to give you understanding, empathy, compassion, forgiveness. Ask Him to show you your part in whatever is irritating you.
- *M&M's.* Chocolate helps just about anything. Buy a one-pound bag, then use these M&M's to give you a clearer picture. Try to think objectively about your spouse's *motive* and your *mood* at the time. In my case, I came to see Dr. Snuggles was simply focused on other things—spending time with kids and grandkids, for instance. (The Mary and Martha [another M&M!] scenario comes to mind.)

Should he have jumped up to help me? Probably. Did he deliberately ignore me? No. He held no vengeful motives and no pre-twenty-first-century views of a woman's place in the home. My mood? Frazzled. This was the first time we'd had family visiting in months. I hadn't done a deep clean since Christmas. I wanted everything to be perfect. I was half of a marital spat waiting to happen.

- *Don't expect your husband to be God.* Statistics may show that marriages fall apart primarily because of financial or sexual issues, but I firmly believe this point is at the heart of the majority of marital conflict. We have expectations, and we want our spouses to love us enough to know them. The problem is, our finite brains aren't equipped with that kind of extrasensory perception. Bottom line: If you want something, ask for it. Nicely, of course. I could have saved myself a week of clenched teeth if I'd just said, "When you have a minute, could you help me with _____?"

As with most issues, communication is the key. In my house, most of our "issues" arise because I think I know what my husband is thinking. I rarely do. It's so easy to misinterpret a facial expression or read layers into a simple comment. Talking to God and then to your man is always a good place to start. If, after doing this, you discern true ill will, it's time to seek wise counsel. For the everyday clashes caused by unrealistic expectations or wrong assumptions, a heart-to-heart talk can usually give a relationship the needed reboot.

Another tip is to think back on the times you have been forgiven by a long-suffering, ever-patient Savior. Loving the way

God does, we'll give our SITH a pass for that unkind remark, and another for forgetting to start the dishwasher, and another for leaving a wet towel on the floor, and another for forgetting what we said three minutes ago . . .

> The minute you shut down the communication about what you need, resentment is a really festering thing when you're sharing space.
>
> —Brené Brown, best-selling author of *Daring Greatly* and *The Gifts of Imperfection*[2]

We'll forgive with generosity and pattern our pardons after the One who pardoned us.

I need to add a PS here. A few weeks after my rant subsided, we went camping with friends. My husband loaded the kayaks into the pickup; attached our bikes to the rack; hooked the camper to the truck; drove two and a half hours; backed us into our site; unhooked the camper; lowered the jacks; leveled the camper; connected the water, electric, and sewer; set up our chairs; pulled out the awning; and grilled supper. And that was just day one. Me? I dozed on the way and made a salad for supper.

Thanks for the pass, honey.

— Cynthia —

Most husbands and wives see, hear, taste, and feel differently. After all these years of marriage, I finally understand one of the reasons my husband has to ask twice what I'm referring to . . . even if I'm pointing at it.

"Wonderhubby, would you mind putting this box over there?"

"Where?"

"The spot I'm pointing to."

"What spot?"

"This one," I say, pointing harder, because that's a thing.

It happened this week. We were both bent over our hardwood floors, replacing damaged floorboards. He asked me where his nail punch was.

"Right here."

"Where?" He looked around the room, his head swiveling.

"Right. Here. I'm holding it out to you, which is why I said 'here.'" Some say snark is my spiritual gift. Well, no one actually says that, but they're probably thinking it.

Why couldn't he see—?

Oh.

The broad bill of his protective and somewhat attractive baseball cap was in the way. And that explains episodes four through forty-eight of the same issue. Not that he volunteered to remove his cap when I was clearly trying to get his attention, but still . . .

On almost every point of contention, disappointment, or misunderstanding in marriage, we have an opportunity to rewrite the sentence, the emotional content, the narrative, and the ending.

Sometimes it's as simple (note: simple, not necessarily easy) as exchanging traditional responses for healthier wording.

Our wording can grow tattered, frayed, worn-out as much as anything that's used frequently. But how often do we consider that words may need to be replaced for better, more efficient, and kinder-to-the-soul options?

"Why don't you ever . . . ?" turns into "I want to understand why . . ."

"That's a stupid idea" turns into "Tell me your reasoning behind doing it that way."

"You don't bring me flowers anymore" turns into "It blesses me when you bring me flowers for no reason other than your love for me."

"Here's what you need to do" turns into "Have you considered . . . ?"

"That won't work" turns into "Is there any way I can help?"

"You're in my way" becomes "Excuse me, my love."

And "I wish you would for once—" becomes silence.

What?

Years ago, I was in the middle of constructing a Pulitzer Prize–worthy sentence something like, "I wish you would for once in your life—" when I heard voices. Well, a voice. A Voice with a capital *V*. Deep in my spirit, I sensed God urging me to go ahead and say what I was about to, but in prayer. Not out loud to my husband or in a growl too low for him to hear, but reshaped into a prayer. I believe God was inviting me to convert my rant into prayer . . . then to leave that prayer in His hands and see what happened.

> I believe God was inviting me to convert my rant into prayer . . . then to leave that prayer in His hands and see what happened.

So I did. Every time I felt a compulsion to complain about something my husband did or failed to do, or whine about how he'd hurt my feelings, or lower myself to begging for what I thought he should know we or I needed, I went silent and in my mind snuck off to convert it into prayer.

"Lord, Wonderhubby isn't catching on that it would mean a lot to me if when I return from a speaking engagement, he would greet me at the door and see if I need help with my luggage. I've mentioned it, with no response. Would you please impress it on his heart without my having to say a word? And if not, then make me less sensitive on that issue. Amen."

God answered both prayers. He made me less sensitive about it, and He moved my husband to—of his own volition (or so he must have thought)—meet me with a hug and reach to help me with my bags.

Coincidence? I stopped believing in coincidences long ago.

When words would bubble to the surface about irritations

large or small, I worked on developing the habit of not letting them escape but instead "saying it in prayer." Soon, I couldn't keep up with the answers. I marveled at how much more effective it was to say it to Jesus than to say it to my husband.

I found myself praying for whatever wound in my husband was at the heart of his words that wounded me, or praying that he would come home from work with energy to spare rather than that God would smite him with the idea that the lawn needed to be mowed.

Aware that God was the One listening to the words I said to *Him* rather than to my husband, I chose kinder words, a gentler approach, and selfless ideas. And that made me choose the same with what I *did* say directly to my husband.

Mercy is an art form. Consider how its beauty can upgrade the atmosphere in your home:

- What's one small mercy you can show your spouse today, whether or not they deserve it?
- What's one large mercy you can demonstrate on an issue that has been a longtime irritation?
- Are there facial expressions, body language, or inflammatory words you're willing to forgo in order to let mercy reign in your household?
- How do your insecurities make you less eager to forgive or show mercy to others? Why do you think we excuse our own unforgiveness because of the hurts in our past?
- If you could eliminate the exhaustion factor, past disappointments, and an overly busy schedule, how much easier would it be for you to apply mercy? What practical steps can you take to not let exhaustion, past disappointments, and a busy schedule call the shots in your home?
- Are you willing to treat offenses not as the last straw but as the first straw in a new batch?

Micah 6:8 says, "He has shown you . . . what is good. And what does the LORD require of you? To act justly and to love mercy and to walk humbly with your God."

To *love* mercy. Love to *apply* mercy. *Opt* for mercy. Make mercy our *default* option.

Sadly—bordering on tragically—we let more than our girths go as we age and our marriages tick off the years. We let our communication skills droop too. And when we see each other a lot, like 24/7, common courtesy suddenly seems like too steep a hill to climb.

I read an article recently about a real-life *Lord of the Flies* group of Tongan boy castaways in 1965 who were marooned on a deserted island for more than a year.[3] Unlike William Golding's characters in the 1954 novel (who ganged up against one another, scarred themselves intellectually and emotionally, and eventually destroyed one another), the Tongan boys made the most of their dire circumstances, showed each other mercy and forgiveness, depended on their faith, and banded together to build and maintain strong relationships. That became the secret to their survival in a harsh, unforgiving environment.

Not saying that working from home or being home all the time with your spouse could turn into a *Lord of the Flies* scenario, but . . .

As I mentioned in an earlier chapter, a few years ago, I pre-forgave my husband for any offenses he might commit in our future together. I don't always *remember* that I pre-forgave him. But God has His ways of jogging my memory.

I didn't invent the idea. Jesus did. He pre-forgave me through His God-designed covenant with me. It wasn't a bargaining chip. I had nothing to offer but a laundry list of mistakes and sins and foul-ups and regrets. When I asked Him to forgive me, He did, and included every offense I would commit in the future (see 1 John 1:9).

So much of navigating marriage is simply implementing what Jesus modeled. If Jesus approaches my relationship with Him from a stance of "I already forgave you for next Tuesday's impatience and that rolling-your-eyes-behind-his-back thing that will crop up a week from tomorrow," isn't that the pattern He would want me to follow with my spouse in the house?

If I give my SITH a pass on that insensitivity he demonstrated ten minutes ago and the replay of it that might happen the next time we both want to shower first, I'm not doing anything magnanimous that might qualify me for wife of the year. Like a musician doing a cover of another band's famous song, I'm singing what Jesus composed and made famous.

> As we've interacted with thousands of couples over the past four years, there is one missing ingredient that causes a marriage to struggle: *grace*. . . .
>
> When grace is missing from a marriage, three words dominate that relationship: You. Owe. Me. . .
>
> So many couples try to correct their behavior or change their communication patterns, but without grace those changes are temporary and exhausting. Grace is the starting point from which all change is made.
>
> —Justin and Trisha Davis, founders of RefineUs
> Ministries and authors of *Beyond Ordinary: When
> a Good Marriage Just Isn't Good Enough*[4]

CHAPTER 20

Continuing the Love Story

— Becky —

Whenever I see a stooped, white-haired couple walking hand in hand, I always respond with, "Oh, they're so cute together. I hope that's us someday." Meaning, I hope we're both here in our nineties, and I really, really hope we're still holding hands.

I want to run up and ask these marriage veterans to share their bliss secrets. Most likely they've been home together 24/7 for years, maybe decades. But they apparently still love each other.

I want to ask, "Did you ever get on each other's nerves? Do you still? How do you resolve conflict? Do you compromise, or does one of you give in all the time? How are you serving each other? Are you still dating? What advice can you give that will help my marriage?"

I've googled "Marriage advice from couples married over fifty years" and even found an article that listed bliss tips from centenarians who'd been together eighty years or more. The line I used to end chapter 17 encompasses almost every sage tidbit: "It's the little things we do that add up to a life lived mostly in step with each other."

Little things. Patience, communication, grace, affection. Every marriage is made up of moments, and those moments are filled with choices. The way I choose to think, feel, or respond in this moment may determine how the rest of the day goes. Decisions fill days and days become years.

Imagine an hourglass flipped upside down the moment we said "I do." We have no control over the speed, but let's pretend we can control the color of the grains of sand.

The way I choose to think, feel, or respond in this moment may determine how the rest of the day goes. Decisions fill days and days become years.

Each grain represents a moment of your married life. Anger, bitterness, sarcasm, unrealistic expectations, nagging, selfishness, criticizing, comparison, envy, and disrespect turn the particles black. Admiration, appreciation, smiles, affectionate touch, words of love and affirmation, acts of service, forgiveness, grace, joy, and gratitude coat the grains in iridescent colors.

What if each of us had an hourglass in the middle of the kitchen table, in full view of anyone who entered our home? What would your centerpiece look like? The bottom of mine would be covered in bright Easter egg colors. Some of the middle layers would be speckled with far more black than I want to look at. But the grains that are sifting through now, thanks partly to the soul-searching necessitated by writing this book, are actually kind of pretty. All because I'm making better choices. Not easy or perfect, but better.

So what does a day in the life of a mostly-happily-home-together-all-the-time couple look like? What are the moments and choices that fill their day? They might look like this. (Don't throw your hands up in despair halfway through. Please hear me out.)

- Praying for your man before getting out of bed, "How can I bless him today, Lord?"

- Brushing your teeth and combing your hair before a morning kiss. Making that kiss linger just a bit.
- Snuggling on the couch and chatting about plans for the day over coffee.
- Choosing to offer your blessing when he says he'd rather go golfing with the guys instead of cleaning the basement with you.
- Reading a daily devotional and praying together.
- Choosing a nice T-shirt over the comfy one with the hole in the shoulder.
- Putting a touch of color on your face even if "no one" will see you today.
- Sitting across from each other in your home office, then happily leaving your work half done at 10 a.m. so he can have the room for his Zoom call.
- Asking a friend to join you for coffee instead of cleaning the basement alone in an angry huff.
- Welcoming, or suggesting, a looong lunch together . . . because choosing blessing over resentment keeps the glow of that lingering morning kiss alive.

I promised to get back to *renewed*, spelled "re-nude" by my not-so-smart phone. Many of us struggle with body image, and our lack of confidence creeps into our feelings about physical intimacy. Years ago, Dr. Snuggles said something that opened my eyes to how my body negativity was affecting him: "You are the only woman I will ever see naked for my entire life. Like the song says, you are 'Every Woman in the World' for me." That hit hard. I'm *it* for him. I have a role to play in helping him guard his heart, mind, and eyes. Have I banished all self-consciousness? No. But it's a goal I'm striving for. I want gifting my husband with all of me to color some of the sand in my hourglass.

—Becky

- Making supper together while catching up on your time apart.
- Dinner by candlelight.
- Taking a walk . . . hand in hand, the way you hope you'll still be doing decades from now.
- Playing a board game and not minding if he wins.
- Sharing a bowl of popcorn during a movie. Action and adventure tonight, rom-com tomorrow. Saying yes to his preference for extra butter—deciding your diet can resume tomorrow.
- Cuddling in bed and saying what you appreciate about each other before a lingering kiss and turning out the lights.
- Thanking God for this man He gave you as you drift off to sleep.

Still with me?

Unrealistic? Absolutely.

Have Dr. Snuggles and I ever floated through a single day with that much lovey-dovey like-mindedness? Nope.

And yet . . .

If I'm choosing blessing over cursing, forgiveness over resentment, a pass over bringing up the past—if I'm asking God, moment by moment, to help me choose grace—some of those warm fuzzies will be part of many of our days, and our life and our love will be mostly good.

So what little things can you choose today? Light a candle at dinner? Do one of his chores before he gets to it? Buy his favorite snack? Tell him he's wonderful?

Sometimes, especially on those meh days, a simple thank-you is all we can muster. But the smile that answers those two words might prevent a nosedive.

Sometimes, saying nothing is the best "little thing." As I write this, we're sharing 260 square feet of camper. He just turned on the TV. While I'm writing. Six feet away. I feel the *grrr* start to rise in my throat, but I stop.

Choose grace. Choose grace. Choose grace.

These words spark to life a little quicker these days. I smile. And grab the chunky yellow earplugs. Once again, a grace choice saved my mood and the moment.

What little thing can you do to make today memorable . . . in a good way?

> Just like a baby doesn't come with an operating manual, neither does a spouse. Spouses, just like kids, are incredibly complex creatures, and every single one is different (and is constantly changing, just to make it a little more of a challenge).
>
> Trying to navigate and please an estrogen-oriented mind with a testosterone-oriented mind is challenging, to say the least, and pretty much impossible in the real world. I frequently haven't a clue what is going on in that female mind (maybe I don't want to know, either), but her happiness is one of my highest priorities in life, so most everything I do is oriented toward that goal.
>
> —Dr. Snuggles

My friend Debbie says, "My husband doesn't like celebrating anniversaries. He feels every day should be date night. Before we started going out, I thought date night had to be doing something like dinner or a movie. He changed my mind and showed me a board game at home or cooking a new recipe can be just as much fun. This mindset helps make being home together easier for us. When the weather is nice, we'll pack a picnic basket full of food (some days we have hot dogs, some days steak and shrimp) and walk out to our patio. My husband lights the firepit as I set the table. We watch the sunset, catch up on our day, and eat a fun meal."

Debbie added, "While catching up with friends, one said, 'It's good to really love who you are married to. We're fortunate.' So true. Those words, along with the popular meme 'I love you more than yesterday . . . Yesterday you got on my nerves,' have been my go-to reminders as we embark on the adventures of life together."

Don't you love that meme? Yesterday you bugged me, but today is a new day and I choose to love you more. What a grace-filled way to start a day . . . or the rest of your marriage.

—— Cynthia ——

A love story in a book draws to a conclusion but never truly to "the end." The characters live on in our imagination after the final page. But every good novelist knows that the story needs to leave the reader with a meaningful takeaway. Because *meaningful* makes *memorable*.

When both spouses are home all the time, learning the new dance steps of 24/7 togetherness isn't the end of their story. They're creating new chapters with every life experience, every challenge, every crisis, every dip, and every kiss.

My twenty-year-old grandchild recently introduced my husband and me to a friend with these words: "They have the cutest love story." Our favorite introduction ever. It wasn't a recitation of what we each did for a living, or our individual gifts, or what we've accomplished in the way culture normally expects. It was better than that. Our grandchild was proud of her grandparents' love story, imperfect as she knew it was.

No matter what subplots blindside a couple, no matter what villains have tried their best to interrupt the quest, no matter what mistakes we've made or regrets we harbor, our love story isn't over yet.

What chapter are you writing now that you're spending most of your time together at home? Does it comfort you—as it does us—to know that you can change the ending, even now?

We can change the dialogue and the narrative of our love stories so they don't crumble in a crisis, dissolve during dilemmas, fade, fizzle, or fall apart. We can reject the subplot of mere tolerance or a sense of martyrdom or silent but growing disappointment. And yet, we don't actually have the power to effect change like that. But we do have access to the One who does.

God is in the transforming business. When the walls feel like they're closing in, even in a good, healthy, strong marriage, he can lead us into "a broad place" (Psalm 18:19 ESV). That place may not be physical—like an open concept living room–dining room–kitchen—but is more likely to be internal.

When we entrust our relationship to the wide-open-places God, He expands the space for the "we" in "We're Home All the Time." The presence of our spouse doesn't have to cramp our style or shrink our safe zone. It can enlarge our capacity for grace, kindness, companionship, growth.

And humor.

> The presence of our spouse doesn't have to cramp our style or shrink our safe zone. It can enlarge our capacity for grace, kindness, companionship, growth.

An hour ago, Wonderhubby and I had one of those word collisions that was supposed to be a conversation. It's as if we were speaking two different languages and forgot each other's sentences as soon as they were spoken, and every tug of a new word made a more complicated tangle. Yes, it had to do with finances, but that's not the point.

We had to remind each other that we were on the same side of this thing called life. Eventually we found the first knot and untangled it. Then the next. Resolution. Way long ago when we were immature, like six months ago, we might have held on to the memory of the tangle rather than the wonder of the resolution.

It's an hour later. I brought him blueberries fresh from the garden. He complimented me on a task I'd completed earlier in the day. I asked if he needed anything. He told me a funny story I hadn't heard him tell before. And we laughed together. The walls of our home resonated with our togetherness laughter. A sweet sound.

Every day, I have a choice: build our relationship word by word, reaction by reaction, response by response, or tear it down. I can opt for resentment or opt for grace. I can set my default to "pre-forgive" or to "hold a grudge." (That button is a magnet for unsightly fingerprints, just so you know.)

> This is the stage of life where your surrounding circumstances bolster love and appreciation in your marriage. As your children, their friends, and even your grandkids get married, their relationships are reminders of how much love God has poured into your marriage over the years. Then as friends begin to lose their mates, and attending funerals and reading obituaries become monthly or weekly activities, our hearts value each day, each hour, each moment together as more and more precious.
>
> —Pam Farrel, speaker and author of
> *A Couples' Journey with God*

Whether our togetherness season is long or too short, how it will read to others and how we'll remember it depend on the choices we make—all eighty trillion of them. We decided "I do." Now we daily decide "I will."

I will watch for opportunities to encourage him.

I will give him breathing room without creating distance.

I will let laughter be the sound our walls—and others—hear in this home.

I will make my love for my spouse obvious.

I will give myself permission to create and protect the space I need, for the sake of our relationship.

I will keep growing in my understanding of how God's Word applies to this season of our marriage.

I will let love win every argument.

I will practice kindness until it's automatic.

I will give my SITH a pass. And another. A lifetime of passes.

I will view this time as a WHATT Club member rather than a HHATT Club member.

And I will cherish the moments that may one day be no more than memories.

Each of us has the ability, by God's grace, to rewrite the narrative of our home through all the seasons and the sweet ending of our love stories. It is never too late to get started with that editing process. A season of unemployment, or caregiving, or retirement, or confinement at home cannot be given permission to mess with our relationship in negative ways. We can invite positive change, though, and determine that even as we learn the dance steps to keep from tripping over each other when we're home together all the time, this clumsy stage of figuring it out won't be how our story ends.

This Is Not How Our Story Ends
by Cynthia Ruchti

The look in your eyes when I tell you I love you,
After all the times when words came so hard,
The warmth of your hand on the pulse of our story,
The miles tick on, and they take us far.
Far from the place where our journey started,
Far from the moment our love derailed,
Wrapped in the grace of a Love undeniable,
The miles tick on, and they take us far.

If I could erase all the tears I caused you,
If you could forget all the tears that were mine,
If all that we said and all we left unsaid
Could fade into memories we'd no longer find,
The path that we've taken, the one we're still traveling,
Miles—steep or smooth—ahead of us now,
Would tell us the journey of love's worth the taking.
We've come so far, but we've so far to go.
With the wind at our back, or against it we're leaning,
When roads lead us higher, or life twists and bends,
I promise you, love, that though riddled, regretted,
With hope, this is not how our story ends.
No, this is not how our story ends.[1]

Acknowledgments

Above all, we thank the One who created man, woman, and matrimony. He gifted us with amazing men, our SITHs, and ordained our WHATT status—and continues to teach us grace, love, mercy, and patience.

Both of us are grateful, too, for our agent, Wendy Lawton, and Books & Such Literary Management for seeing the value in this project, and for Kregel Publications and their team's vision for it. Thank you for shepherding it well and blessing us with your kindness and expertise.

— Cynthia —

Within my wingspan are friends, family, and fellow writers who inspire me every day. If you look closely, between the lines of this book are the fingerprints of those who lifted each word in prayer.

My siblings and their spouses live out the concept of godly love in their grace-filled marriages. Thanks for modeling *forever* for future generations.

Becky, it's been a joy to coauthor with you. Let's do it again soon! Far beyond that, though, I need to thank you for being one of those friends who makes me a better woman, a better wife, and a better follower of Jesus.

— Becky —

Thank you to my sons and their wives for your support and encouragement and for providing great examples of intentional relationships for this book. Scott and Kristen, Jeff and Holly, Aaron and Adrianne, Mark and Brittany, I have learned so much from the way you love your spouses well.

I am so grateful for the friends who offered anecdotes, asked often how the writing was progressing, and lifted *Spouse in the House* before the throne of grace in prayer. Thank you, Tuesday Night Study, Upper Room Ladies, Crossway Communicators, LifeBridge Circle, and Fill My Cup, Lord Writers. I am so blessed by your steadfast presence in my life.

Cynthia, I am honored and blessed to call you my sister in Christ. I love being on this writing journey with you. Thank you for listening, making me laugh, and flat-ironing my emotional flyaways.

We would both like to express our deep gratitude to everyone who shared their stories of trials and victories, and to those who graciously offered input from their years of professional and ministry experience to enrich this addition to the marriage-and-togetherness conversation. Your wisdom, counsel, and advice have been invaluable.

If Your Spouse Is a Louse
(When Home Is Not a Safe Place)

We have intentionally kept much of this book lighthearted because, for the majority of marriages where differences in communication styles and unrealistic expectations create glitches in our happily-ever-after software, the right mixture of humor and grace can reboot, rewire, and repair most of our problems. But if you are one of the nearly five million women in the United States experiencing abuse from an intimate partner, our hearts go out to you.

With spiritual, medical, and psychiatric intervention, some abusers can be rehabilitated and some formerly unsafe relationships can transform into marriages operating out of love and respect. But it is always imperative to separate from the abuser if there is a danger of harm to you or your children. Breaking free from an unsafe relationship can seem impossible, but there is hope. Here are some steps and resources that can help.

> Create a practical plan that allows you to remain safe now, while you're planning to leave, and after you leave.

The National Domestic Violence Hotline recommends that you create a practical plan that allows you to remain safe now, while you're planning to leave, and after you leave. The following steps are often helpful:

- Tell a safe person. Call a hotline or local professional or talk to a trusted friend.

- Record instances of abuse, including pictures and medical records, and hide them in a safe place.
- Research local shelters and ask about resources before you need them in a crisis.
- Make a list of what you will need to bring with you: driver's license, birth certificate and children's birth certificates, social security cards, money and/or credit cards (in your name), checking and/or savings account books, emergency numbers, medical records, etc.
- Consider online job training that will help you find a job after you leave.
- If you can set aside some money, ask a trusted friend or relative to hold it for you.
- Be aware that you can request a police escort when it is time to leave.

Hotlines

National Domestic Violence Hotline: https://www.thehotline .org/, 1-800-799-SAFE (7233) or TTY 1-800-787-3224

Focus Ministries: Faith-based domestic violence help for women and families, https://www.focusministries1.org, 630-617-0088

National 24-Hour Women of Substance Crisis Intervention Hotline: 1-866-862-2873

Ministries

Peace and Safety in the Christian Home: https://godsword towomen.org/pasch.htm

FaithTrust Institute: www.faithtrustinstitute.org

Books

The Battered Wife by Nancy Nason-Clark

The Verbally Abusive Relationship: How to Recognize It and How to Respond by Patricia Evans

Violence in Families: What Every Christian Needs to Know by Al Miles

When Dad Hurts Mom: Helping Your Children Heal the Wounds of Witnessing Abuse by Lundy Bancroft

Why Does He Do That? Inside the Minds of Angry and Controlling Men by Lundy Bancroft

———

Our prayer is that God will lead you to people who can come alongside you to help in this difficult time.

May God's opinion of you, and your trust in Him, lift your heart this hour.

> I have loved you with an everlasting love; I have drawn you with unfailing kindness. (Jeremiah 31:3)

> And may you have the power to understand, as all God's people should, how wide, how long, how high, and how deep his love is. May you experience the love of Christ, though it is too great to understand fully. Then you will be made complete with all the fullness of life and power that comes from God. (Ephesians 3:18–19 NLT)

> God has said, "Never will I leave you; never will I forsake you." (Hebrews 13:5)

> There is no fear in love, but perfect love casts out fear. (1 John 4:18 ESV)

Top Ten Questions to Help SITHs Find Their Footing

1. What matters more to you than the health of your marriage and the person you married?

2. If your answer made you uncomfortable, sit quietly and consider how you can shift priorities. What is within your power, with God's help, to change so the next time you're asked that question, you're pleased with your answer?

3. What one creative idea can you implement today to ensure your home is a true haven for any who enter, and especially for your spouse?

4. Even if your spouse is "the" problem, are you willing to participate with God in finding solutions?

5. Would you describe your home as chaotic, noisy but fun, or a place of calm? How would your spouse answer that question?

6. Among your friends, whose influence strengthens your marriage? How?

7. Among your friends, whose influence stirs up dissatisfaction or unrealistic expectations in your marriage? Why are you keeping company with that person?

8. Proverbs 14:1 says, "The wise woman builds her house, but with her own hands the foolish one tears hers down." What habits, practices, or traditions make your house look more like demolition day than restoration day?

9. What are three or four of your core values? What are three

or four of your spouse's core values? Where do they intersect, and how can you maximize those important connections?

10. Which slogan will you choose for the next season of your lives together?

Grace always gets the last word.
Love wins.
What can I do to help?
Welcome home.

Inspiration for Any
Home-All-the-Time Circumstance

DAILY FAMILY TO-DO LIST

LAUGH TOGETHER.

CRY TOGETHER.

GET ANGRY. IT HAPPENS.

GRIEVE TOGETHER.

BE GRATEFUL. SAY IT OUT LOUD.

STRUGGLE WITH EACH OTHER.

SORT LIES FROM TRUTH.

BINGE ON SOMETHING GOOD.

FAST FROM SOMETHING, TOO.

WORK TOGETHER ON SOMETHING THAT'S HARD.

PLAY.

REST.

HUG.

PRAY.

HELP EACH OTHER.   loveisfearless.com

Inspiration for Conversations
with One Another

"Fear-talk" is like an emotional fever.
It's an indication that
we need healing.

loveisfearless.com

LOVE-talk:	**FEAR-talk:**
Affirmation	Ridicule
Respect	Blame
Storytelling	Shame
Encouragement	Panic & drama
Healthy humor	Cutting sarcasm
Conflict resolution	Trash talk
Empathy	Flattery
Impact & influence	Silent treatment
for good	All the stuff that comes
Disagreement paired	with codependency,
with authentic	passive aggression,
listening	and gaslighting

Resources for Consideration

Classic Marriage: Staying in Love as Your Odometer Climbs by Michelle Rayburn with Phil Rayburn

Men Are Like Waffles, Women Are Like Spaghetti: Understanding and Delighting in Your Differences by Bill and Pam Farrel

"Nerds and Free Spirits Can Unite over the Budget" by Dave Ramsey, https://www.daveramsey.com/blog/nerds-and-free-spirits-can-unite-over-the-budget

Reimagining Your Love Story: Biblical and Psychological Practices for Healthy Relationships by Andrea Gurney

Staying Power: Building a Stronger Marriage When Life Sends Its Worst by Carol and Gene Kent and Cindy and David Lambert

This Life We Share: 52 Reflections on Journeying Well with God and Others by Maggie Wallem Rowe

Notes

Chapter 1: Honey, I'm Home . . . All. The. Time.

1. Cynthia Ruchti, *Song of Silence* (Nashville: Abingdon, 2016), 120.

Chapter 2: Love Keeps No Record of Who Cleaned the Toilet Last

1. Marco Bertoni and Giorgio Brunello, "*Pappa Ante Portas*: The Effect of the Husband's Retirement on the Wife's Mental Health in Japan," *Social Science and Medicine* 175 (February 2017): 135–42, https://doi.org/10.1016/j.socscimed.2017.01.012.

Chapter 6: But Honey, Both Our Names Are on the Mortgage

1. Norman Jewison, dir., *Fiddler on the Roof* (Burbank, CA: Mirisch Company, 1971).

Chapter 7: At Least One of Us Has to Be a Bomb Sniffer

1. Varun Warrier et al., "Genome-Wide Meta-Analysis of Cognitive Empathy: Heritability, and Correlates with Sex, Neuropsychiatric Conditions and Cognition," *Molecular Psychiatry* 23 (2018): 1402–409, https://www.nature.com/articles/mp2017122.
2. Grant Hilary Brenner, "When Is Porn Use a Problem?," Psychology Today, February 19, 2018, https://www.psychologytoday.com/us/blog/experimentations/201802/when-is-porn-use-problem.
3. "Gambling Statistics: Gambling Stats from Around the World," Gambling.net, accessed June 17, 2021, https://www.gambling.net/statistics.php.

Chapter 8: The Sins Febreze Can't Quite Cover

1. C. S. Lewis, *Mere Christianity* (San Francisco: HarperOne, 2009), 115.
2. This is an excerpt from a *Heartbeat of the Home* radio script Cynthia Ruchti wrote and produced.

Chapter 9: We're Dancing, but He's Listening to Different Music

1. "USFS General Dance Rules & Regulations," San Diego Figure Skating Communications, 2011, http://iceskatingresources.org/DanceGeneralRules.html.
2. "Torvill & Dean Bolero – 1984 Olympic Winning Routine," Vienna81, February 1, 2008, video, 8:34, https://youtu.be/E8obUdxnTlc.
3. The chewing gum king's original words were "When two men always agree, one of them is unnecessary." See Neil M. Clark, "Spunk Never Cost a Man a Job Worth Having," *American Magazine* 111 (March 1931): 63.

Chapter 10: Are We Renting or Owning This Marriage?

1. *Merriam-Webster Online*, s.v. "vow," accessed June 17, 2021, https://www.merriam-webster.com/dictionary/vow.
2. Jill Briscoe, "Breaking Free from Sexual Temptation," Telling the Truth, March 28, 2016, https://www.tellingthetruth.org/read/individual-post/read/2016/03/28/breaking-free-from-sexual-temptation.
3. Linda J. Waite and Maggie Gallagher, *The Case for Marriage: Why Married People Are Happier, Healthier and Better Off Financially* (New York: Broadway Books, 2001), 75.

Chapter 12: Get That Out of My Pail! (His Bucket List Doesn't Play Well with Mine)

1. Kristen Melby, "Filling the Bucket . . . ," *Norskehuvia* (blog), May 1, 2020, https://www.norskehuvia.com/blog/filling-the-bucket.
2. Melby, "Filling the Bucket . . ."

Chapter 13: It's Still My Rib, Adam. It's Still My Rib Cage, Eve.

1. "Without You (Badfinger Song)," Wikipedia, last modified June 13, 2021, https://en.wikipedia.org/wiki/Without_You_(Badfinger_song).

Chapter 14: Why We Need HHATT Sisters and Guys Need Guy Friends

1. E. J. Mundell, "Science Quiets Myth of 'Chatterbox' Females," ABC News, March 24, 2008, https://abcnews.go.com/Health /Healthday/story?id=4507818&page=1.

2. Róisín Parkins, "Gender and Emotional Expressiveness: An Analysis of Prosodic Features in Emotional Expression," *Griffith Working Papers in Pragmatics and Intercultural Communication* 5, no. 1 (2012): 46–54, https://www.griffith.edu.au/__data/assets /pdf_file/0026/363680/Paper-6-Parkins-Gender-and-Emotional -Expressiveness_final.pdf.

3. Mundell, "Science Quiets Myth of 'Chatterbox' Females."

4. *Strong's Exhaustive Concordance*, s.v. "chaber," BibleHub, accessed June 17, 2021, https://biblehub.com/hebrew/2270.htm.

Chapter 16: Familiarity Breeds Meh

1. Stacy Lee, "Ways for Couples to Connect During Shelter in Place," Couples Institute Counseling Services, April 8, 2020, https:// couplesinstitutecounseling.com/ways-for-couples-to-connect -during-sheltering-in-place/.

Chapter 18: I Meant It When I Said "I Do" to the "In Sickness" Part of Our Vows

1. Lexico, s.v. "grace," accessed June 17, 2021, https://www.lexico .com/en/definition/grace.

Chapter 19: Give Your SITH a Pass

1. Oswald Chambers, "The Distraction of Contempt," My Utmost for His Highest, accessed June 17, 2021, https://utmost.org /the-distraction-of-contempt/.

2. Brené Brown, "Why Discomfort and Vulnerability Are Important," *CBS This Morning*, March 30, 2020, https://www.cbs.com/shows /cbs_this_morning/video/BSOQ98PabUo_ixvMgb5wwQsV EsGRatww/why-discomfort-and-vulnerability-are-important/.

3. Jesse Mulligan, "The True Story of Six Tongan Teenage Castaways in 1965," RNZ, May 15, 2020, https://www.rnz.co.nz/national /programmes/afternoons/audio/2018746636/the-true-story-of-six -tongan-teenage-castaways-in-1965.

4. Justin and Trisha Davis, "One Thing That Changes Every Marriage," *RefineUs* (blog), RefineUs Ministries, December 2, 2013, http:// refineus.org/one-missing-ingredient/.

Chapter 20: Continuing the Love Story

1. Originally published in Cynthia Ruchti, *Miles from Where We Started* (Wheaton, IL: Gilead, 2018). The recorded version, with vocals by Aaron Herman, guitar by Chet Stevens, mastering by Eric Wolf of Wolf Mastering, and mix by Sal Salvador, can be found at https:// www.cynthiaruchti.com/miles-from-where-we-started-songs/.

Don't miss Cynthia Ruchti's award-winning fiction!

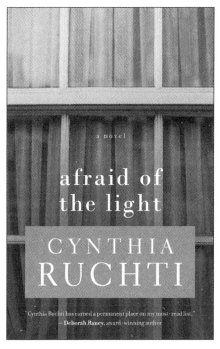

"Ruchti's best work yet."
—*Publishers Weekly*, starred review

"Filled with heartfelt moments and dynamic characters."
—*Woman's World*, This Week's Best New Books pick

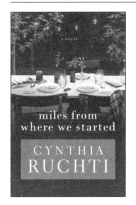

"With her dry humor and grace-filled insight, Ruchti crafts another story that tickles the funny bone even as she speaks to the soul. . . . A profoundly moving story not to be missed."
—*Hope by the Book*

CynthiaRuchti.com